Angels In The Kitchen

CAJUN HOSPICE-TALITY

HOSPICE FOUNDATION OF ACADIANA, INC.

Angels in the Kitchen
CAJUN HOSPICE-TALITY

Published by Hospice Foundation of Acadiana, Inc.
Copyright © 2006
Hospice Foundation of Acadiana, Inc.
2600 Johnston Street, Suite 236
Lafayette, Louisiana 70503-3240
(337) 237-1332
fax (337) 266-5565
www.hfacadiana.com

Paintings © Cover Jeffrey J. Joseph, MD; page 11 Jebbye Moroux; page 29 Shann Comeaux;
page 63 Daren Tucker; page 97 Paul Schexnayder; page 131 Laura Laborde;
Page 165 Chuck Broussard; page 199 Bonnie Camos

ISBN: 0-9768323-0-5

Edited, Designed, and Manufactured by
CommunityClassics™

An imprint of

FRP™

P.O. Box 305142
Nashville, Tennessee 37230
(800) 358-0560

Manufactured in China
First Printing: 2006   5,000 Copies
Second Printing: 2007   6,000 Copies

Acknowledgments

We would like to thank the following Chair-Angels for their countless hours of commitment to this wonderful project:

Becky Credeur (Chair-Angel)
Becky Berthelot (Co-Chair-Angel)
Andrea Doucet (Sponsor/Marketing Chair-Angel)
Betty Ellison (Testing Chair-Angel)
Roger Laurent (Angel Art Collection)
Mike Blanchard (Non-Recipe/Story Angel Editor)
Kent Hutslar (Angel Art Photographer)

We would also like to thank the following Angels for volunteering to be testing captains, typists, and general help in this endeavor. To all the other testing Angels and anyone else who assisted in this project, we thank you.

Acadiana Women   *Margie Castille*   *Kelly LeVine*
Peggy Alciatore   *Sue Cole*   *Juliet McKay*
Elizabeth Badeaux   *Hazel Delahoussaye*   *Jan Mickey*
Hilda Begnaud   *Sandra Duhon*   *Dee Patin*
Barbara Bird   *Carolyn Fontenot*   *Ra Nelle Simon*
Ann Black   *Jan Greer*   *Pat Wright*
Jennifer Bordelon   *Linda Larkan*
Lisa Breaux   *Janice LeBlanc*

About the cover

COVER ART: JEFFREY J. JOSEPH, M.D.—*A TASTE OF HEAVEN ON EARTH*
Submitted in Memory of Emile Joseph

When not performing his art on the human face as a facial, plastic, and reconstructive surgeon, Dr. Joseph furthers his innate creativity through oil painting. He enjoys portraits painted loosely, as well as graphic art.

About Hospice of Acadiana, Inc.

Hospice of Acadiana, Inc., is a non-profit organization of compassionate, well-trained professionals, support staff, and volunteers who provide a comprehensive program of medical care, counseling, and spiritual direction to persons with life-threatening conditions and their families. Founded in March of 1983, we have the longest record of continuous service of any hospice in the state of Louisiana. The administrative office of Hospice of Acadiana, Inc., is located in Lafayette, Louisiana, but care is provided in patients' homes, nursing homes, and hospitals throughout our service area. That service area includes the civil parishes of Acadia, Iberia, Lafayette, St. Landry, St. Martin, St. Mary, and Vermilion—the heart of the French-speaking region of Louisiana known as Acadiana.

When Hospice of Acadiana, Inc., was established, one of the guiding principles—in addition to a commitment to compassionate care for the dying—was a pledge to accept all medically eligible patients, regardless of their ability to pay for services. Through the efforts of the Hospice Foundation of Acadiana, Inc., and projects such as this cookbook, we have been faithful to that pledge. In addition, we have distinguished ourselves by broadening our family of services in end-of-life care, even when there is no direct payment source involved. Among those programs are our Center For Loss and Transition, Camp Brave Hearts, Heart Prints, and Improving Care.

An underlying principle of the hospice philosophy is that the entire family, not just the patient, is the unit of care. For that reason, one phase of hospice services does not even begin until after the patient's death. That phase is the bereavement program—offered through our Center For Loss and Transition and designed to help family members cope with the loss of their loved one. Included among the bereavement services offered by Hospice of Acadiana, Inc., is Camp Brave Hearts, a summer day camp for grieving children ages 7–12.

To more effectively respond to the needs of children from birth to age 19 living with a life-threatening condition, Hospice of Acadiana, Inc., developed a model of care that offers alternatives to the traditional hospice approach. Such a model for a pediatric palliative program minimizes the emotional barriers to accepting services and maximizes the benefit to patients and family members alike. That program is known as Heart Prints. And for adult patients diagnosed with a life-threatening condition but with a life expectancy of more than six months, we have developed the Improving Care program.

Medical, psycho-social, and spiritual needs of patients and their families are addressed by a specially qualified interdisciplinary team of Hospice staff members, with an emphasis on keeping the patient at home with family and friends as long as possible. The care team at Hospice of Acadiana, Inc., includes physicians and registered nurses certified in hospice and palliative care. The team consists of the following members:

- A volunteer medical director

- Volunteer physicians who make home visits

- Registered nurses

- Certified home health aides

- Professional social workers

- Chaplains

- Bereavement counselors

- A registered pharmacist

- Physical therapists

- Massage therapists

- A registered dietitian

- Volunteers

Table of Contents

Introduction

Volunteers of the Hospice Foundation of Acadiana, Inc., have lovingly and diligently assembled this collection of recipes, anecdotes, and words of wisdom with a three-fold purpose in mind:

- To increase public awareness of Hospice of Acadiana, Inc.,

- To raise funds in support of Hospice of Acadiana, Inc., and

- To offer lasting tribute in memory of patients cared for by Hospice of Acadiana, Inc.

The idea of using a cookbook to achieve those goals is not unusual in the area served by our hospice and from which we have taken our name. Warm-hearted hospitality and the enjoyment of well-seasoned foods are vital parts of the *joie de vivre* in the French-speaking region of Louisiana known as Acadiana.

Nor is the concept alien to the philosophy of hospice itself. As one might guess, the word "hospice" is derived from the same root that gives us "hospitality." In the case of a home-based program such as hospice, however, the roles of host and guest are often interchangeable. We frequently speak of admitting patients into our care; in that sense, they become our guests. It is equally true, though, that we are daily allowed privileged admission into the homes and lives of our patients and their families.

Hospice caregivers, both professional and volunteer, are often called "angels of mercy" by our patients. Once again, though, it is we who are also fed, nurtured as we are by the faith, courage, and wisdom of patients facing the end of life. They are angels-in-the-making who have glimpsed the heavenly world to which we all aspire and messengers from a country beyond time, where there is no more death, nor sorrow, nor crying, nor pain. It is almost as though the writer of Exodus were speaking to us caregivers when he wrote, "See, I am sending an angel ahead of you to guard you along the way and to bring you to the place I have prepared. Pay attention to him and listen to what he says." The wisdom of those angels—reflected in the stories and inspirational sayings that are a key ingredient of this collection—has added flavor to our lives, no less than Cajun seasoning does to a good étouffée.

Such is the nature of hospice work and, indeed, the nature of all unselfish caring for others: that in giving we ourselves are doubly blessed. That is a truth discovered and shared by Lewis Bernard, a petroleum landman by profession and a hospice volunteer. About his first visit to a new patient, he reflects:

> *After some cordial remarks, I asked him, "So how are you doing with your situation?" and he responded, "Why, this is what I have lived my life for. This is what I have been waiting for." And I said to myself, WOW. What a man. A real man who really understood what his faith was all about. He was literally dying to meet his maker. No fear, nothing held back, ready to go. He was so at peace with himself. What a lesson for me. You know, we read about this, others talk about it, but here was a real man in front of me, dying and very close to his death, actually living out his faith. I was happy for him, and there was no doubt that he had lived his life full of love and for this moment. If only I could be so well prepared for that moment.*

It is to such angels that we dedicate this collection, *Angels in the Kitchen: Cajun Hospice-tality.*

Acknowledgment of Sponsors

SERAPHIM DIAMOND

Stephen Domingue—*In memory of my loving Uncle Patrick Domingue*

Andrea Credeur Doucet—*In memory of my loving husband, Kermit A. Doucet, and my father, Russell Credeur*

Guy Ellison, Jr.—*In memory of E. W. Wynne III and Mrs. Ruth Falk*

Louisiana Oncology Associates

Marnel Pharmaceutical, Inc.—*In recognition of the physicians who donate their time and talent to Hospice of Acadiana, Inc.*

Acadian Ambulance Service

SERAPHIM GOLD

Barry and Becky Berthelot—*In memory of Mr. and Mrs. F. X. Berthelot, Albin Major and Van Major*

Dr. Shirley Covington—*In memory of Norma Thompson*

Kergan Bros., d/b/a Sonic Drive-In

J. P. Thibodeaux Inc.—*In memory of J. P. Thibodeaux*

SERAPHIM SILVER

Tara and André Doucet—*In memory of their poppa, Kermit A. Doucet, and their grandfather, Russell Credeur*

Dr. Michel Heard

Ann Knight—*In memory of Eddie Knight*

Gregory and Carol Long—*In memory of Ann and Earl Downs*

Dr. A. N. McCallum

John and Jan Mickey—*In memory of Dr. Joe Mickey and Johnny DiLeo*

Tommy and Deidre Montgomery, Forrest, Madison, Carver, and Oakley—*In memory of Denbo Montgomery, M.D.*

Morgan Keegan

Oncologics, Inc.

Dave and Mary Romagosa—*In memory of Dr. and Mrs. Jerome Romagosa*

Premier Medical Equipment

Professional Arts Pharmacy—*In memory of Dr. W. I. "Bill" Smith and Leslie Lancon*

Urology Associates of Lafayette

Wally Broussard—*In memory of Vivian D. Porter*

Brunch and Breads

LIFE'S RECIPE

One cup of good thoughts.
One cup of kind deeds.
One cup of consideration for others.
Two cups of sacrifice for others.
Three cups of forgiveness.
Two cups of well-beaten faults.

Mix ingredients thoroughly and add tears of joy and sorrow and sympathy for others. Fold in four cups of prayer and faith to lighten other ingredients and raise the texture to great heights of Christian living. After pouring all into your daily life, bake well with the heat of kindness and serve with a smile.

—Barbara Mouton

ARTIST: JEBBYE MOROUX—"TONY ANGEL"
Submitted in loving memory of her husband Tony Moroux, father
Judge Jerome Domengeaux, and nephew Eraste Autin.

Jebbye is a well-known artist throughout the Acadiana area. Through the untimely death of her husband, her home burning down one Christmas Eve, and a brain hemorrhage, she has continued to smile, love life and paint.

Breakfast Casserole

10 slices bread, crusts removed and bread
   cut into cubes
1¹/2 pounds bulk pork sausage, cooked,
   drained and crumbled
12 ounces shredded Cheddar cheese
5 eggs
2 cups milk
³/4 teaspoon dry mustard
1 (10-ounce) can condensed
   cream of mushroom soup
¹/2 cup milk

Spread the bread cubes in the bottom of a baking dish. Top with the sausage and
sprinkle with the cheese. Beat the eggs, 2 cups milk and the dry mustard in a bowl.
Pour evenly over the sausage mixture. Cover and chill overnight. Mix the mushroom
soup and ¹/2 cup milk in a bowl. Pour over the cheese layer. Bake, uncovered, at
350 degrees for 1¹/2 to 2 hours.

Serves 6

THE TRAGEDY OF LIFE IS NOT THAT WE DIE, BUT THAT WE FAIL TO

MAKE THE MOST OF THE TIME BETWEEN BIRTH AND DEATH.

—*W. I. "Bill" Smith, M.D.*

crawfish quiche

1 unbaked (9-inch) pie shell
1 tablespoon butter
1 pound crawfish tails
1 tablespoon Cajun seasoning
1 garlic clove, minced
1 cup chopped onion
1/2 cup chopped green bell pepper
1/4 cup finely chopped tasso
1/2 cup (2 ounces) shredded Swiss cheese
3 eggs
1 cup heavy cream or half-and-half

Prick the pie shell with a fork. Bake at 350 degrees for 5 to 10 minutes or until lightly browned. Remove to a wire rack. Melt the butter in a saucepan. Add the crawfish and Cajun seasoning. Sauté until the liquid evaporates. Add the garlic, onion, bell pepper and tasso. Sauté over low heat until the vegetables are tender. Spoon into the pie shell. Sprinkle with the Swiss cheese. Beat the eggs and cream in a bowl. Pour over the cheese. Bake at 350 degrees for 30 minutes or until the center springs back when lightly touched.

Serves 4 to 6

Mushroom and Onion Quiche

1 1/2 cups all-purpose flour
3/4 teaspoon salt
1/4 cup (1/2 stick) margarine
1/4 cup shortening
2 1/2 tablespoons milk
8 slices bacon
1 cup thinly sliced onion
8 ounces sliced mushrooms
1 cup sour cream
3 eggs, beaten
3/4 teaspoon salt
1/8 teaspoon white pepper
1 1/2 teaspoons chopped green onions

Sift the flour into a bowl. Stir in 3/4 teaspoon salt. Cut in the margarine and shortening with a pastry blender or fork until the mixture resembles coarse crumbs. Sprinkle with the milk. Stir with a fork just until the mixture holds together. Shape into a ball. Roll out on a lightly floured work surface to fit a 9-inch pie plate. Fit into the pie plate and flute the edges. Prick the pastry with a fork. Bake at 425 degrees for 10 to 12 minutes or until golden brown. Remove to a wire rack. Cook the bacon in a skillet until crisp. Remove to paper towels to drain; crumble. Add the onion and mushrooms to the bacon drippings. Sauté until the vegetables are tender. Mix the sour cream, eggs, 3/4 teaspoon salt, the white pepper and green onions in a large bowl. Stir in the mushroom mixture and bacon. Pour into the pie shell. Bake at 300 degrees for 30 minutes.

Serves 8

Spinach Bacon Quiche

6 slices bacon, crisp-cooked and crumbled
1 unbaked (9-inch) pie shell
1 cup (4 ounces) shredded Swiss cheese
4 eggs
1 (10-ounce) package frozen chopped spinach,
*   thawed and well drained*
1 tablespoon all-purpose flour
1/2 teaspoon salt
1/4 teaspoon nutmeg
2 cups heavy cream
Cayenne pepper to taste

Sprinkle the bacon in the pie shell. Top with the cheese. Mix the eggs, spinach, flour, salt and nutmeg in a bowl. Stir in the cream and season with cayenne pepper. Pour into the pie shell. Bake at 375 degrees for 40 minutes or until golden brown and set.

Serves 6 to 8

Gourmet Breakfast Health Drink

2 1/2 ounces soft tofu
3/4 cup soy milk
1 carrot, chopped
3/4 cup chopped fruit such as apple,
*   banana, peach or blueberries*
3/4 cup orange juice
2 tablespoons wheat germ
2 tablespoons wheat bran
2 tablespoons flax seed

Purée the tofu, soy milk, carrot, fruit, orange juice, wheat germ, wheat bran and flax seed in blender.

Serves 2 or 3

Crawfish-Stuffed Bread

1/2 cup (1 stick) butter
2 garlic cloves, minced
1 onion, chopped
1 bell pepper, chopped
1 pound crawfish tails, finely chopped
1 cup chopped green onion tops
1/2 teaspoon crushed basil
1 teaspoon chopped jalapeño chiles
Creole seasoning to taste
3 (1-pound) loaves frozen bread dough,
    thawed for 5 hours
4 ounces mild Cheddar cheese, shredded
Melted butter

Melt 1/2 cup butter in a large saucepan. Add the garlic, onion and bell pepper.
Sauté for 10 to 15 minutes. Add the crawfish, green onion tops, basil and jalapeño
chiles. Season with Creole seasoning. Sauté for 5 minutes. Remove from the heat.
Roll out 1 loaf of dough to a 10×20-inch rectangle on a lightly floured work
surface. Cut in half to make 2 squares. Spread 3/4 cup of the crawfish mixture over
one end of one square. Sprinkle with 2 to 3 tablespoons of the cheese. Roll up
tightly, folding in the edges as you roll to seal. Place gently on a nonstick baking
sheet, making certain all edges are tightly sealed. Repeat with the remaining bread
dough, crawfish mixture and cheese to make 6 rolls. Bake at 375 degrees for
20 minutes or until golden brown. Remove to a wire rack and immediately brush
with melted butter. Serve hot.

Serves 30

NOTE: This bread freezes well. Cool and wrap tightly in foil before freezing.

Ham and Cheese Finger Rolls

1¹/2 cups (3 sticks) margarine, softened
3 tablespoons mustard
3 tablespoons poppy seeds
1 onion, finely chopped
1 teaspoon Worcestershire sauce
18 Philly-style hoagie rolls
12 ounces shaved ham
10 to 11 ounces shaved Swiss cheese

Mix the margarine, mustard, poppy seeds, onion and Worcestershire sauce in a bowl. Split the rolls horizontally. Spread the margarine mixture on the inside of the rolls. Arrange the ham and cheese on the bottom half of the rolls. Replace the tops of the rolls. Cut each roll into 4 slices. Wrap 6 of the sliced rolls in foil to seal. Repeat with the remaining rolls. Bake at 350 degrees for 25 minutes.

Serve 72.

NOTE: These rolls freeze well. Bake for 45 minutes, if frozen.

THE GREATEST GIFT YOU CAN GIVE TO SOMEONE YOU LOVE IS TO

ALLOW THEM TO CARE FOR YOU IN YOUR LAST DAYS.

—W. I. "Bill" Smith, M.D.

Sausage Bread

2 pounds ground beef
1 pound ground pork
1 large onion, chopped
1 bell pepper, chopped
2 teaspoons chopped garlic
2 loaves frozen bread dough, thawed
¹/2 cup (1 stick) butter, softened
8 ounces green olives
4 ribs celery, chopped
16 ounces Swiss cheese, shredded
16 ounces Cheddar cheese, shredded

Brown the ground beef and ground pork with the onion, bell pepper and garlic in a skillet, stirring until the meat is crumbly; drain. Cut each loaf of bread dough into thirds. Roll out each third 12 inches across on a lightly floured work surface to a 12-inch rectangle. Spread with the butter. Spread the meat mixture evenly over the dough. Top with the olives and celery. Sprinkle with the Swiss cheese and Cheddar cheese. Roll up and seal the seams. Place seam side up on a nonstick baking sheet. Bake at 350 degrees for 30 to 45 minutes or until golden brown.

Serves 36

NOTE: This bread freezes well. Bake at 350 degrees for 15 minutes. Cool and wrap in foil before freezing. Bake at 350 degrees for 30 to 45 minutes.

Stuffed Bread

8 ounces ground beef
8 ounces ground pork
1/2 cup chopped onion
1/3 cup chopped bell pepper
2 ribs celery, chopped
2 green onions, chopped
2 garlic cloves, minced
1 teaspoon paprika
Cajun seasoning to taste
1 (12-ounce) can refrigerator French
bread dough
1 cup (4 ounces) shredded favorite cheese

Brown the ground beef and ground pork in a skillet, stirring until the meat is crumbly; drain. Stir in the onion, bell pepper, celery, green onions, garlic and paprika. Season with Cajun seasoning. Cook until the vegetables are softened. Unroll the bread dough on a nonstick baking sheet. Spread the meat mixture over 1/2 of the bread. Sprinkle with the cheese. Fold the bread over the meat mixture and pinch the edges to seal. Bake at 350 degrees for 30 minutes.

Serves 4 to 6

Italian Biscotti

5 1/3 tablespoons butter or margarine, softened
2/3 cup sugar
1 tablespoon baking powder
2 eggs
1 teaspoon vanilla extract or other flavoring
2 cups all-purpose flour
1/3 cup chopped nuts (optional)
1 egg yolk (optional)
1 tablespoon water (optional)

Beat the butter in a large bowl with an electric mixer at medium speed for 30 seconds. Beat in the sugar and baking powder. Beat in the eggs and vanilla. Beat in as much of the flour as possible until too stiff for the beaters. Stir in the remaining flour and the nuts. Divide the dough in half and chill until the dough is easy to handle. Shape each half into a 9-inch log. Place 4 inches apart on a lightly greased baking sheet. Flatten each log slightly to 2 inches wide. Beat the egg yolk and water in a small bowl. Brush on the logs for a shiny surface. Bake at 375 degrees for 25 to 30 minutes or until a wooden pick inserted in the center comes out clean. Cool on the baking sheet for 1 hour. Remove to a cutting board. Cut diagonally with a serrated knife into 1/2-inch slices. Arrange the slices, cut side down, on an ungreased baking sheet. Bake at 325 degrees for 8 to 10 minutes. Turn the slices over and bake for 8 to 10 minutes longer or until dry and crisp. Remove the cookies to a wire rack to cool. Store in an airtight container at room temperature for 2 days or in the freezer for up to 6 months.

Serves 32

VARIATION: To make amaretto biscotti, use almond extract instead of vanilla and add 3 to 4 teaspoons of amaretto to the dough.

Sailor Biscuits

4 cups buttermilk baking mix
1 cup sour cream
3/4 cup club soda
2 tablespoons margarine, softened
1/2 cup (1 stick) margarine, melted

Combine the baking mix, sour cream and club soda in a bowl. Stir just until combined. Turn out onto a floured work surface and knead 10 times. Cut into 16 large biscuits using a biscuit cutter. Grease a baking pan with 2 tablespoons margarine. Arrange the biscuits in the prepared pan. Brush 1/4 cup of the melted margarine over the biscuits. Bake at 400 degrees for 20 to 22 minutes. Remove to a wire rack. Brush the remaining 1/4 cup melted margarine over the hot biscuits.

Serves 16

Whole Wheat Biscuits

1 cup whole wheat flour
1 cup unbleached all-purpose flour
1 tablespoon baking powder
1 teaspoon salt
1 tablespoon brown sugar
1/2 cup (1 stick) butter
1 egg, beaten
2/3 cup milk

Mix the whole wheat flour, all-purpose flour, baking powder, salt and brown sugar in a bowl. Cut in the butter with a pastry blender or fork until the mixture resembles coarse crumbs. Stir in the egg and milk. Roll out on a floured work surface to a 10×16-inch rectangle. Fold 1/3 of the dough in and then fold in the other 1/3. Turn the dough and roll out to a 10×16-inch rectangle. Repeat 3 or 4 times. Cut with a biscuit cutter and place the biscuits on an ungreased baking sheet. Bake at 450 degrees for 12 to 15 minutes.

Serves 12

Decadent French Toast

1 cup packed brown sugar
2 tablespoons corn syrup
5 tablespoons butter
8 slices French bread
5 eggs
1¹/₂ cups milk
1 teaspoon vanilla extract
Sour cream and fruit for topping

Combine the brown sugar, corn syrup and butter in a saucepan. Cook until bubbly, stirring often. Pour evenly into a 9×13-inch baking pan. Fit the bread slices in a single layer on top of the brown sugar mixture. Beat the eggs, milk and vanilla in a bowl. Pour over the bread. Cover and chill overnight. Bake, uncovered, at 350 degrees for 45 minutes. Loosen from the sides of the pan with a sharp knife and cut between the bread slices to separate. Invert onto a platter so that the caramel mixture is on top. Place on individual serving plates and top with sour cream and fruit. Serve immediately before the caramel hardens.

Serves 8

WE TEND TO DIE THE WAY WE LIVE. AND HOW WE DIE

WE WILL LIVE FOREVER.

—*Fr. Michael Champagne, CJC*

Banana Fritters

1 cup all-purpose flour
2 teaspoons baking powder
1 heaping tablespoon sugar
1 scant teaspoon salt
3/4 cup milk
6 to 8 bananas, sliced
Vegetable oil for frying
Confectioners' sugar

Mix the flour, baking powder, sugar and salt in a bowl. Add the milk and stir to
mix well. Stir in the bananas. Drop by spoonfuls into hot oil in a saucepan. Cook
until golden brown on both sides. Remove to paper towels to drain. Sprinkle with
confectioners' sugar and serve hot.

Serves 4 to 6

DO NOT NEGLECT TO SHOW HOSPITALITY TO

STRANGERS, FOR BY DOING THAT SOME HAVE ENTERTAINED

ANGELS WITHOUT KNOWING IT.

—Hebrews 13:2

Quick Beer Bread

3 cups self-rising flour
1/2 cup sugar
1 (12-ounce) can beer
1/4 cup (1/2 stick) butter or
  margarine, melted

Sift the flour and sugar into a bowl. Stir in the beer. Pour into a lightly greased 5×9-inch loaf pan. Bake at 350 degrees for 45 minutes or until a wooden pick inserted in the center comes out clean. Remove to a wire rack and pour the melted butter over the top.

Serves 8

WHOEVER IS HAPPY WILL MAKE OTHERS HAPPY TOO. HE WHO HAS

COURAGE AND FAITH WILL NEVER PERISH IN MISERY.

—Anne Frank

Broccoli Corn Bread

2 (8-ounce) packages corn bread mix
1 small onion, chopped
1 small carton cottage cheese
2 teaspoons Tabasco sauce
1 (10-ounce) package frozen chopped
  broccoli, thawed
4 eggs, beaten
1 cup (2 sticks) margarine, melted
1 can whole kernel corn, drained (optional)

Combine the corn bread mix, onion, cottage cheese, Tabasco sauce, broccoli, eggs, melted margarine and corn in a large bowl. Stir to mix well. Pour into a greased 9×13-inch baking pan. Bake at 350 degrees for 1 hour or until a wooden pick inserted in the center comes out clean. Remove to a wire rack to cool.

Serves 6 to 8

IF YOU HAVE THE GUTS TO FACE YOUR GRIEF, GOD WILL

GIVE YOU THE GRACE TO LIVE BEYOND YOUR LOSS

—*Joan T. Broussard*

Mexican Corn Bread

1 cup cornmeal
1/4 cup all-purpose flour
1 teaspoon salt
1 teaspoon baking soda
3/4 cup cubed Velveeta cheese
1/3 cup vegetable oil
1 (14-ounce) can cream-style corn
3/4 cup milk
2 eggs, beaten
2 hot chiles, seeded and finely chopped
1 onion, chopped

Mix the cornmeal, flour, salt and baking soda in a large bowl. Add the cheese, oil, corn, milk, eggs, chiles and onion. Stir to mix well. Pour into a nonstick 10×14-inch baking pan. Bake at 350 degrees for 30 minutes or until a wooden pick inserted in the center comes out clean and the top is lightly browned. Remove to a wire rack to cool.

Serves 12

YOU MATTER TO THE LAST MOMENT OF YOUR LIFE,

AND WE WILL DO ALL WE CAN, NOT ONLY TO HELP YOU DIE

PEACEFULLY, BUT TO LIVE UNTIL YOU DIE.

—*Dame Cicely Saunders, founder of the modern hospice movement*

French Bread San Marcos

1 cup mayonnaise
1/2 teaspoon Worcestershire sauce
1 to 2 dashes of Tabasco sauce, or to taste
2 cups (8 ounces) shredded Cheddar cheese
1 cup (4 ounces) shredded Monterey Jack cheese
1/2 cup finely chopped onion
1/4 cup (1/2 stick) butter, softened
1 loaf French bread
1/2 to 1 cup grated Parmesan cheese
Paprika

Combine the mayonnaise, Worcestershire sauce, Tabasco sauce, Cheddar cheese, Monterey Jack cheese and onion in a bowl. Stir to mix well. Cut the bread in half lengthwise. Spread with the butter. Spread the cheese mixture over the bread. Sprinkle with the Parmesan cheese and paprika. Place on a baking sheet. Bake at 300 degrees for 30 minutes. Place under a broiler until golden brown, watching closely to avoid burning.

Serves 8

Appetizers and Beverages

My Mom loved ministering to others. She cooked meals and brought flowers from her garden to those who needed food or cheering up. She even visited prisoners in the jail. She ran errands for the housebound. If someone needed help, my Mom was there. When she developed lung cancer, we were devastated. But Mom said to her family, "Well, if someone had to get it, I'm glad it was me and not any of you."

Mom continued being active in her church and serving others. Even as her health declined and her cancer spread to her bones, she refused to indulge in self pity. She used her walker to go to a neighbor's house each evening to wash her dishes because the neighbor had a broken arm. As Christmas neared, Mom knew that this would be her final one. She was busy making handcrafted gifts for her family and friends. When I visited with her one weekend as she struggled to complete those gifts, she shared with me that for several months she had been seeing an angel dressed in blue. He never spoke to her; he would just suddenly appear. "What do you think it means?" she asked. I didn't think that my mother was having hallucinations. She was perfectly lucid, and besides, I believed in angels—they were in the Bible, after all. Why couldn't God send one to be with Mom in her final weeks? And that's what I said to Mom. "I think it means that God has sent you a heavenly companion to accompany you as you prepare to leave this world." The "Blue Angel" continued to be with my mother until she left this world on New Year's Day, surrounded by her loved ones. On her tombstone are angels with these words from the book of Psalms: "For he shall give his angels charge over you, to keep you in all your ways. In their hands, they shall bear you up." (91:11-12)

—*Pat Lejeune, R.N.*

ARTIST: SHANN COMEAUX—"ANGEL FOOD,
$\frac{1}{2}$ CUP SPICE & $\frac{1}{2}$ CUP HEAVEN"
Submitted in memory of Millie Comeaux Moreau

In addition to using different paints and media, Shann uses a burning match as a paintbrush, as was done with the piece submitted. She was very moved to submit an angelic piece of art from an experience she had as a kindergarten teacher. She would say the rosary to herself on a regular basis as the children were napping. Looking up at the ceiling she noticed a water stain. Over time, the water stain got bigger, year after year. One day, looking up, she noticed it had formed a perfectly symmetrical shape of an angel!

Craw-Pouches

8 ounces cream cheese, softened
3 jars marinated artichoke hearts,
*   drained and chopped*
2 cups (8 ounces) shredded sharp Cheddar cheese
1 red bell pepper, finely chopped
1 bunch green onions, chopped
Few dashes of Tabasco sauce
1 package won ton wrappers
1 pound crawfish tails

Combine the cream cheese, artichokes, Cheddar cheese, bell pepper, green onions and Tabasco in a bowl. Stir to mix well. Separate the won ton wrappers on a work surface. Spray each wrapper with nonstick cooking spray. Place 1 teaspoon of the cheese mixture in the center of each wrapper. Top each with 1 crawfish tail. Bring the corners of the wrapper to the center to form a pouch. Place in greased miniature muffin cups. Bake at 325 degrees for 15 minutes.

Serves 50

TEACH US TO NUMBER OUR DAYS ARIGHT, THAT

WE MAY GAIN A HEART OF WISDOM.

—*Psalm 90:12*

Crawfish Boulettes

2 pounds crawfish tails, chopped
1 bell pepper, chopped
1 rib celery, chopped
1/2 cup chopped green onions
1/2 to 3/4 cup (1 to 1 1/2 sticks) butter, softened
1/2 teaspoon cayenne pepper
Creole seasoning to taste
1 cup bread crumbs

Combine the crawfish, bell pepper, celery, green onions, butter and cayenne pepper in a bowl. Season with Creole seasoning. Stir to mix well. Shape into balls and roll lightly in the bread crumbs. Arrange on a baking sheet. Bake at 400 degrees for 20 minutes.

Serves 8 to 10

A GOOD CHARACTER IS THE BEST TOMBSTONE. THOSE WHO
LOVED YOU AND WERE HELPED BY YOU WILL REMEMBER YOU WHEN
FORGET-ME-NOTS HAVE WITHERED. CARVE YOUR NAME
ON HEARTS, NOT ON MARBLE.

—*Charles H. Spurgeon*

Shrimp Toast

1 pound deveined peeled shrimp
1 onion, chopped
1 (1/2-inch) piece fresh ginger, peeled
*   and chopped*
1/2 teaspoon salt
Large pinch of freshly ground pepper
2 egg whites
30 (1×3-inch) strips thinly sliced bread,
*   crusts removed*
1/2 cup fine fresh bread crumbs
Light vegetable oil for frying

Combine the shrimp, onion, ginger, salt and pepper in a food processor or blender. Process until finely chopped. Add the egg whites with the machine running and process until well mixed. Spread the shrimp mixture 1/4-inch thick on the bread strips. Dip the shrimp side into the bread crumbs to coat. Place on a baking sheet, shrimp side up. Cover with plastic wrap and chill. Heat oil 1 1/2 to 2 inches deep to 360 degrees in a large skillet. Add the shrimp bread and fry until golden brown on both sides. Remove to paper towels to drain. Serve hot.

Serves 30

NOTE: These may be frozen before frying. Remove from the freezer and carefully add to the hot oil to fry.

Shrimp in Cream Sauce

6 tablespoons butter
1/2 cup all-purpose flour
1 teaspoon salt
1/4 teaspoon white pepper
2 cups milk
2 cups (8 ounces) shredded American cheese
1 pound fresh deveined peeled medium shrimp

Melt the butter in a saucepan over low heat. Stir in the flour, salt and pepper. Cook for a few minutes, stirring constantly. Remove from the heat and stir in the milk. Return to the heat and cook until thick, stirring constantly. Add the cheese and shrimp. Cook for 10 minutes or until the shrimp turn pink, stirring often. Remove to a chafing dish and keep warm. Serve over toast points or melba rounds.

Serves 4 to 6

NOTE: You may spoon the shrimp mixture into ramekins and top with bread crumbs. Bake at 350 degrees until bubbly.

Coconut Shrimp with Sweet Dipping Sauce

2 pounds fresh large shrimp (about 48)
1 1/2 cups all-purpose flour
1/2 teaspoon baking powder
1/2 teaspoon paprika
1/2 teaspoon curry powder
1/4 teaspoon salt
1/4 teaspoon cayenne pepper
1 (12-ounce) can beer
1/2 cup all-purpose flour
1 (14-ounce) package flaked coconut
Vegetable oil for deep-frying
Sweet Dipping Sauce (below)

Peel and devein the shrimp, leaving the tails attached. Mix 1 1/2 cups flour, the baking powder, paprika, curry powder, salt and cayenne pepper in a bowl. Stir in the beer. Dredge the shrimp in 1/2 cup flour. Coat in the batter and roll in the coconut. Heat oil in a heavy saucepan or deep-fryer to 350 degrees. Add the shrimp and fry until golden brown on all sides. Remove to paper towels to drain. Serve with Sweet Dipping Sauce.

Serves 12

Sweet Dipping Sauce

1 (10-ounce) jar orange marmalade
3 tablespoons horseradish
3 tablespoons Creole mustard

Combine the marmalade, horseradish and Creole mustard in a bowl. Stir to mix well.

Tamale Balls

1 pound ground beef
1 pound bulk pork sausage
1 1/2 cups white cornmeal
2 teaspoons chili powder
2 teaspoons cumin
1 teaspoon salt
1 teaspoon cayenne pepper
3/4 cup vegetable juice cocktail
1/2 cup all-purpose flour
4 garlic cloves, minced, or 1 teaspoon
  garlic powder
Sauce (below)

Combine the ground beef, sausage, cornmeal, chili powder, cumin, salt, cayenne pepper, vegetable juice cocktail, flour and garlic in a bowl. Stir to mix well. Shape into small balls and arrange in a large baking pan. Pour the Sauce over the tamale balls. Bake at 300 degrees for 2 hours or until cooked through, stirring gently after 1 1/2 hours.

Serves 32

NOTE: These can be made ahead and frozen.

Sauce

5 cups vegetable juice cocktail
2 teaspoons chili powder
2 teaspoons cumin
2 teaspoons salt

Combine the vegetable juice cocktail, chili powder, cumin and salt in a bowl. Stir to mix well.

Sun-Dried Tomato Pesto Torta

1/2 cup oil-pack sun-dried tomatoes
8 ounces cream cheese, softened
1/2 cup (1 stick) butter, softened
3 tablespoons prepared pesto
1 jar pine nuts

Process the tomatoes in a food processor or blender until finely chopped. Drain the tomatoes, reserving 3 tablespoons of the oil. Press the tomatoes into the bottom of a 2-cup serving dish or two 1-cup serving dishes. Combine the cream cheese, butter, pesto and 2 tablespoons of the reserved tomato oil in a food processor or blender. Process to mix well. Spoon evenly over the tomato layer. Cover and chill for 8 hours. Loosen from the side of the dish with a sharp knife and invert onto a serving platter. Top with the pine nuts and drizzle with the remaining 1 tablespoon of tomato oil. Serve with water crackers.

Serves 12

LIFE IS NOT MEASURED BY THE NUMBER OF BREATHS WE TAKE,

BUT BY THE MOMENTS THAT TAKE OUR BREATH AWAY.

—George Carlin

Italian Stuffed Artichokes

3 artichokes
1 loaf dry French bread, ground into crumbs, or
* 1 container bread crumbs*
3 ribs celery, finely chopped
9 garlic cloves, minced
1 large handful parsley, chopped
1 cup (4 ounces) grated fresh Parmesan cheese
Salt and pepper to taste
1/4 cup white vinegar
Extra-virgin olive oil

Clean the artichokes and trim off the tips of the leaves. Remove the stems. Place in a bowl. Cover with water and let soak. Mix the bread crumbs, celery, garlic, parsley and cheese in a bowl. Season with salt and pepper. Remove the artichokes from the water and drain. Stuff the artichokes with the bread crumb mixture, starting from the inside. Fit the artichokes tightly together upright in a saucepan. Add 3 inches of water and the vinegar to the saucepan. Drizzle the artichokes with olive oil. Cook, covered, over medium heat for 1 1/2 hours or until the leaves pull out easily.

Serves 10 to 12

Delicious Dolmos

1¼ cups olive oil
4 onions, chopped
2 bunches green onions, sliced
1 garlic bulb, minced
6 Roma tomatoes, diced
1 cup pine nuts, lightly toasted
1 tablespoon ground allspice
½ cup dried mint flakes
Salt and pepper to taste
2 bunches parsley, chopped
2 cups rice
80 grape leaves
2 cups chicken broth
1¼ cups lemon juice
2 tablespoons dried mint flakes

Heat ½ cup of the olive oil in a large saucepan. Add the onions, green onions and garlic. Sauté just until the vegetables are tender. Stir in the tomatoes and pine nuts. Stir in the allspice and ½ cup mint. Season with salt and pepper. Cook over low heat for a few minutes. Stir in the parsley. Cook for a few minutes longer. Remove to a large bowl. Stir in the rice; cool. Rinse the grape leaves and drain. Spread the grape leaves on a work surface. Place about 1 tablespoon of the rice mixture on each grape leaf. Roll up tightly. Arrange the rolled grape leaves in 1 very large saucepan or 2 large saucepans. Mix the chicken broth, 1 cup of the lemon juice and ½ cup of the olive oil in a bowl. Pour over the grape leaves. Bring to a boil. Cover and reduce the heat. Simmer over low heat for 30 minutes. Turn off the heat and let cool in the saucepan. Remove the stuffed grape leaves to a large serving platter. Whisk the remaining ¼ cup olive oil, remaining ¼ cup lemon juice and 2 tablespoons mint in a small bowl. Season with salt and pepper. Drizzle over the stuffed grape leaves.

Serves 80

Slow-cooked Mushrooms

4 pounds mushrooms
2 cups (4 sticks) butter
4 cups burgundy
2 cups boiling water
4 chicken bouillon cubes
4 beef bouillon cubes
4$^{1}/_{2}$ teaspoons Worcestershire sauce
1 teaspoon dill seeds
1 teaspoon pepper
1 teaspoon garlic powder
2 teaspoons salt (or to taste)

Combine the mushrooms, butter, burgundy, boiling water, chicken bouillon cubes, beef bouillon cubes, Worcestershire sauce, dill seeds, pepper and garlic powder in a large saucepan. Bring to a slow boil over medium heat, stirring occasionally. Reduce the heat and cover. Simmer for 5 to 6 hours. Cook, uncovered, for 3 to 5 hours or until the liquid barely covers the mushrooms. Stir in the salt. Remove from the heat and let cool. Serve hot in a chafing dish.

Serves 12

NOTE: This freezes well. You may use butter-flavored granules instead of the butter and serve in a serving dish instead of chafing dish.

Mushroom Logs

8 ounces cream cheese, softened
3 green onions, chopped
1 (4-ounce) can mushrooms,
 drained and chopped
1 tablespoon seasoned salt or ranch
 salad dressing mix
Dash of lemon pepper
Dash of cayenne pepper
2 (8-count) cans refrigerator crescent rolls

Combine the cream cheese, green onions, mushrooms, seasoned salt, lemon pepper and cayenne pepper in a bowl. Stir to mix well. Unroll the crescent dough on a work surface. Press the seams between 2 rolls to seal to make 8 rectangles. Spread evenly with the cheese mixture. Roll up from the long side and pinch the edges to seal. Chill until firm. Cut the logs into 1/2-inch slices. Arrange on an ungreased baking sheet. Bake at 375 degrees for 10 to 12 minutes or until golden brown.

Serves 48

NOTE: The unbaked logs can be wrapped well and frozen.

Tortilla Rolls

8 ounces cream cheese, softened
1 cup sour cream
1 (4-ounce) can chopped black olives, drained
1 (4-ounce) can chopped green chiles, drained
1 cup (4 ounces) shredded Cheddar cheese
1/3 cup chopped green onions
Minced garlic to taste
5 to 6 large flour tortillas

Mix the cream cheese and sour cream in a bowl until smooth. Stir in the olives, green chiles, Cheddar cheese and green onions. Season with garlic. Spread on the tortillas. Roll up the tortillas and wrap in plastic wrap. Chill for 2 to 4 hours. Cut into 1/2-inch slices and arrange on a serving platter. Serve with salsa for dipping.

Serves 10 to 12

VARIATION: You may substitute chopped jalapeño chiles for the olives.

I KNOW GOD WILL NOT GIVE ME ANYTHING I CAN'T HANDLE.

I JUST WISH THAT HE DIDN'T TRUST ME SO MUCH.

—Mother Theresa

Blue Cheese Puffs

16 ounces cream cheese, softened
1 cup mayonnaise
1 tablespoon finely chopped onion
1/4 cup finely chopped chives
4 ounces blue cheese, crumbled
1 teaspoon cayenne pepper
1 loaf thinly sliced whole wheat bread
Paprika

Mix the cream cheese and mayonnaise in a bowl until smooth. Stir in the onion, chives, blue cheese and cayenne pepper. Cut rounds from the bread slices using a 1 1/2- to 2-inch biscuit cutter. Spread 1 tablespoon of the cheese mixture on each bread round. Arrange on a baking sheet and freeze until firm. Bake at 350 degrees for 15 minutes. Sprinkle with paprika and serve immediately.

Serves 60

NOTE: The frozen puffs may be stored in freezer bags before baking.

Praline Brie Roll

1 (8-count) can refrigerator low-fat crescent rolls
1 large round Brie cheese, rind removed
2 pralines

Unroll ½ of the crescent dough on a nonstick baking sheet and press the seams to seal. Place the Brie in the center and top with the pralines. Unroll the remaining ½ of the crescent dough on a work surface and press the seams to seal. Place over the cheese and pralines and press the edges to seal. Bake according to the crescent dough directions or until golden brown. Serve with apple slices and crackers.

Serves 10 to 12

SOME DAY, AFTER WE HAVE MASTERED THE WIND, THE
WAVES, THE TIDE AND GRAVITY, WE SHALL HARNESS FOR GOD
THE ENERGIES OF LOVE.

—*Pierre Teilhard de Chardin*

crab Dip

1/2 cup (1 stick) margarine
1 cup chopped onion
1/2 cup chopped bell pepper
1/2 cup chopped celery
1 1/2 cups crab meat
Salt and black pepper to taste
Cayenne pepper to taste
16 ounces cream cheese

Melt the margarine in a saucepan. Add the onion, bell pepper and celery. Sauté until the vegetables are tender. Stir in the crab meat. Cook over medium heat until the liquid evaporates, stirring constantly. Season with salt, black pepper and cayenne pepper. Add the cream cheese and reduce the heat. Cook until the cream cheese melts, stirring often. Serve with crackers.

Serves 60

ADVERSITY IS THE DIAMOND DUST WITH WHICH

HEAVEN POLISHES ITS JEWELS.

—Robert Leighton

Shrimp Dip

8 ounces cream cheese, softened
2 tablespoons mayonnaise
1 can shrimp, drained and liquid reserved
1/2 cup chopped celery
1/2 cup chopped bell pepper
1/2 cup chopped onion
1 teaspoon chopped garlic
1 jalapeño chile, seeded and chopped
1 tablespoon sweet pickle relish
Salt and pepper to taste

Mix the cream cheese and mayonnaise in a bowl until smooth. Stir in the shrimp. Add the celery, bell pepper, onion, garlic and jalapeño. Stir to mix well. Add the pickle relish and season with salt and pepper. Stir to mix well. Add some of the reserved shrimp liquid if the mixture seems too dry.

Serves 4 to 6

NOTE: You may use 8 ounces of deveined, peeled cooked shrimp instead of 1 can of shrimp.

Artichoke Dip

2 cups Hellmann's mayonnaise

2 cups (8 ounces) grated Parmesan cheese

*2 (4-ounce) cans chopped green
    chiles, drained*

*1 (14-ounce) can artichoke hearts,
    drained and chopped*

2 large garlic cloves, minced

2 tablespoons chopped black olives (optional)

2 tablespoons chopped tomatoes (optional)

Combine the mayonnaise, cheese, green chiles, artichokes and garlic in a large bowl.
Stir to mix well. Spoon into a baking dish. Sprinkle with the olives and tomatoes.
Bake at 350 degrees for 25 to 35 minutes. Serve with white corn chips.

Serves 10 to 12

FEAR CAN HOLD YOU PRISONER. HOPE CAN SET YOU FREE.

—The Shawshank Redemption

Black Bean Dip

2 (15-ounce) cans black beans
2 (10-ounce) cans tomatoes with green chiles
16 ounces cream cheese, softened
8 ounces shredded Cheddar cheese

Pour the black beans and tomatoes with green chiles into a colander. Let drain well. Spread the cream cheese in a shallow baking dish. Top with the drained bean mixture. Sprinkle with the cheese. Bake at 350 degrees for 20 minutes. Serve with corn chips.

Serves 24

Spicy Corn Dip

3 (11-ounce) cans niblet corn, drained
1 cup mayonnaise
1 cup sour cream
1/2 bunch green onions, chopped
2 (4-ounce) cans chopped green chiles
1 cup (4 ounces) shredded Cheddar cheese
1/4 cup chopped jalapeño chiles
1 cup mild salsa
8 to 10 dashes of cumin
Salt and pepper to taste

Mix the corn and mayonnaise in a large glass bowl. Add the sour cream, green onions, green chiles, cheese, jalapeño chiles, salsa and cumin in the order given, stirring after each addition. Season with salt and pepper. Cover and chill for 24 hours. Serve with corn ships.

Serves 16 to 20

Mushroom Dip

1 tablespoon butter
1 pound sliced mushrooms
³/4 cup chopped green onions
³/4 cup mayonnaise
6 ounces cream cheese, softened
10 slices bacon, crisp-cooked and crumbled
¹/2 cup (2 ounces) shredded mozzarella cheese
Creole seasoning to taste
¹/4 cup dried parsley flakes

Melt the butter in a skillet. Add the mushrooms and green onions and sauté for 5 minutes. Stir in the mayonnaise, cream cheese, bacon and mozzarella cheese. Season with Creole seasoning. Spread in a quiche dish and sprinkle with the parsley. Bake at 350 degrees for 20 to 25 minutes. Serve with corn chips, crackers or bite-size raw vegetables.

Serves 8

HOPE IS THE POWER OF BEING CHEERFUL IN CIRCUMSTANCES

WHICH WE KNOW TO BE DESPERATE.

—*G. K. Chesterton*

Spinach and Artichoke Dip

1/2 cup (1 stick) butter
1 onion, chopped
1/2 cup chopped green onions
4 garlic cloves, minced
2 (14-ounce) cans artichoke hearts,
* drained and chopped*
1 (10-ounce) package frozen chopped spinach,
* thawed, rinsed and well drained*
8 ounces cream cheese, softened
3 cups sour cream
1 1/2 cups (6 ounces) shredded mixed favorite cheeses
Cajun seasoning to taste
Salt and pepper to taste
1/2 cup (2 ounces) shredded mozzarella cheese

Melt the butter in a large saucepan. Add the onion, green onions and garlic and sauté until the vegetables are tender. Stir in the artichokes and spinach. Add the cream cheese, sour cream and 1 1/2 cups cheese. Stir to mix well. Season with Cajun seasoning, salt and pepper. Pour into a baking dish and sprinkle with the mozzarella cheese. Bake at 350 degrees for 30 minutes.

Serves 8 to 12

Layered Italian Dip

1/3 cup pitted kalamata olives, drained
1 (16-ounce) jar marinated
   artichoke hearts, drained
1/3 cup roasted red peppers, drained
1 cup oil-pack sun-dried tomatoes,
   drained
8 ounces cream cheese, softened
4 ounces feta cheese
6 tablespoons butter, softened
1 tablespoon Italian seasoning
1 cup (4 ounces) grated Parmesan cheese
1/4 cup chopped green onions

Spread the olives, artichoke hearts, red peppers and tomatoes on paper towels to drain and then chop. Process the cream cheese, feta cheese, butter and Italian seasoning in a food processor to mix well. Spray a 4-cup straight-sided bowl with nonstick cooking spray. Line with enough plastic wrap to hang over the outside. Spread 1/2 of the Parmesan cheese in the bowl and top with 1/2 of the tomatoes. Spread 1 cup of the cream cheese mixture over the tomatoes. Top with the red peppers, then the green onions, then the olives, then the artichokes and then the remaining tomatoes. Spread with the remaining cream cheese mixture and sprinkle with the remaining Parmesan cheese. Fold the plastic wrap over the top and press gently to compact the layers. Chill until firm. Lift the mixture from the bowl and invert onto a serving plate. Remove the plastic wrap. Serve with crackers.

Serves 32

NOTE: This can be made in two 2-cup containers. Freeze one container for future use.

Feta and Blue Cheese Dip

1 cup sour cream
2 ounces feta cheese, crumbled
3 ounces light cream cheese, softened
1/2 teaspoon sage
1/2 teaspoon minced garlic
1/2 teaspoon pepper
1/4 teaspoon basil
1/4 teaspoon thyme
3 ounces blue cheese, crumbled

Combine the sour cream, feta cheese, cream cheese, sage, garlic, pepper, basil and thyme in a bowl or food processor. Beat or process to mix well. Stir in the blue cheese.

Serves 16

Tennis Team Cheese Spread

2 cups (8 ounces) finely shredded Cheddar cheese
2 cups pecans, finely chopped
1 bunch green onions, chopped
1 cup mayonnaise
1 jar hot pepper jelly

Combine the cheese, pecans, green onions and mayonnaise in a bowl. Stir to mix well. Shape into a ball. Cover and chill for at least 2 hours. Flatten the cheese mixture on a serving plate. Spread the jelly over the top. Serve with crackers.

Serves 10 to 12

Warm Roasted Pepper and Artichoke Spread

1 cup (4 ounces) grated Parmesan cheese
¹/2 cup fat-free mayonnaise or salad dressing
8 ounces cream cheese, softened
1 small garlic clove, minced
1 (14-ounce) can artichoke hearts,
   drained and finely chopped
1 (7-ounce) jar roasted red peppers,
   drained and finely chopped

Process the Parmesan cheese, mayonnaise, cream cheese and garlic in a food processor fitted with a steel blade. Remove to a bowl. Stir in the artichokes and red peppers. Spread in an ungreased 9-inch pie plate or shallow baking dish. Bake at 350 degrees for 20 to 30 minutes or until heated through. Serve warm with crackers or bite-size raw vegetables.

Serves 24

WE HAVE TASTED THIS BITTERSWEET FOOD WE CALL

GRIEF. . .THE AFTERTASTE OF LOVE SHARED WITH SOMEONE WHO IS NO

MORE. THE PRICE OF BEING LOVED AND OF LOVING, SUCH A FINE

LINE BETWEEN HAPPINESS AND GRIEF.

—Joan T. Broussard

Avocado Corn Salsa

3 or 4 ears fresh corn
6 Roma tomatoes, diced
1 small red onion, diced
3 avocados, diced
3/4 to 1 bunch cilantro, chopped
1/4 cup lime juice
1/2 teaspoon crushed red pepper
Salt to taste

Cut the kernels from the corn using a sharp knife and place in a bowl. Add the tomatoes, onion, avocados, cilantro, lime juice and crushed red pepper. Season with salt and toss gently to mix. Serve with tortilla chips.

Serves 48

NOTE: If made ahead, add the avocados just before serving. You may use frozen corn kernels if fresh corn is not available.

WE DO NOT RECEIVE WISDOM; WE MUST DISCOVER IT WITHIN
OURSELVES AFTER A JOURNEY THROUGH THE WILDERNESS
WHICH NO ONE ELSE CAN MAKE FOR US, WHICH NO ONE CAN SPARE
US, FOR OUR WISDOM IS THE POINT OF VIEW FROM WHICH WE
COME, AT LAST, TO REGARD THE WORLD.

—Marcel Proust

Black Bean Salsa

1 (15-ounce) can black beans, rinsed and drained
1 (15-ounce) can Shoe Peg corn, rinsed and drained
1 (10-ounce) can tomatoes with green chiles
1 small onion, finely chopped
1 bell pepper, chopped
3 tablespoons lime juice
2 tablespoons red wine vinegar
Salt and pepper to taste

Combine the black beans, corn, tomatoes with green chiles, onion, bell pepper, lime juice and vinegar in a bowl. Season with salt and pepper. Toss to mix. Serve with tortilla chips.

Serves 8 to 12

WORRY DOES NOT EMPTY TOMORROW OF ITS SORROW;

IT EMPTIES TODAY OF ITS STRENGTH.

—*Corrie Ten Boom*

Mango Salsa

1 tablespoon vegetable oil
2 tablespoons white wine vinegar
2 tablespoons lime juice
1 tablespoon brown sugar
1/2 teaspoon salt
1/4 cup finely chopped cilantro
2 tablespoons finely chopped purple onion
1 cup finely chopped mango
1/3 cup finely chopped green bell pepper
1/3 cup finely chopped red bell pepper

Whisk the oil, vinegar, lime juice, brown sugar, salt and cilantro in a bowl. Add the onion, mango, green bell pepper and red bell pepper. Toss to mix. Cover and chill for several hours. Serve with tortilla chips.

Serves 4 to 6

VARIATION: Sauté shrimp in garlic and place on flour tortillas. Top with **Mango Salsa and roll up.**

YOU CANNOT DO A KINDNESS TOO SOON, FOR YOU NEVER

KNOW HOW SOON IT WILL BE TOO LATE.

—Ralph Waldo Emerson

Sangría

1 (12-ounce) can frozen limeade
   concentrate, thawed
1 (12-ounce) can frozen lemonade
   concentrate, thawed
1 (12-ounce) can frozen orange juice
   concentrate, thawed
1 (750-milliliter) bottle rosé
1 (750-milliliter) bottle burgundy
3 tablespoons brandy
Club soda

Mix the limeade concentrate, lemonade concentrate, orange juice concentrate, rosé, burgundy and brandy in a large pitcher. Cover and chill. Pour into glasses and add club soda to taste.

Serves 12

NOTE: You may freeze the sangria. Spoon the frozen mixture into glasses and add club soda to taste.

Swamp Breeze

1 (6-ounce) can frozen lemonade concentrate
1 cup spiced rum
³/4 cup dark rum
¹/3 cup orange liqueur
2 or 3 fresh mint sprigs

Process the lemonade concentrate, spiced rum, dark rum and orange liqueur in a blender until smooth. Add ice cubes to the 5-cup fill line. Process until smooth. Add the mint and process to mix well. Pour into glasses and garnish with additional mint sprigs.

Serves 5

LIFE IS MADE UP OF SMALL PLEASURES. HAPPINESS IS MADE
UP OF THOSE TINY SUCCESSES. THE BIG ONES COME TOO
INFREQUENTLY. AND IF YOU DON'T COLLECT ALL OF THESE TINY
SUCCESSES, THE BIG ONES DON'T REALLY MEAN ANYTHING.

—Norman Lear

Hurricanes

1¹/₄ cups light rum
1¹/₄ cups dark rum
1 (46-ounce) can red fruit punch
1 (12-ounce) can frozen orange juice
* concentrate, thawed*
2 (6-ounce) cans frozen lemonade or
* limeade concentrate, thawed*
2 cups pineapple juice
Orange slices and maraschino cherries

Mix the light rum and dark rum in a large pitcher. Add the punch, orange juice concentrate, lemonade concentrate and pineapple juice. Stir to mix well. Cover and chill. Serve over ice and garnish with orange slices and maraschino cherries.

Serves 12

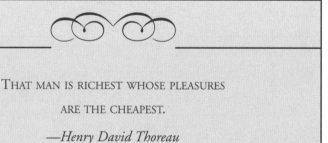

THAT MAN IS RICHEST WHOSE PLEASURES

ARE THE CHEAPEST.

—Henry David Thoreau

Bellinis

1 (10-ounce) can frozen peach concentrate
$1/2$ can vodka
$1/4$ can peach schnapps
Champagne

Combine the peach concentrate, vodka and schnapps in a blender. Add ice and blend until smooth and thick. Spoon into glasses and top with champagne.

Serves 4

WHEN I WAS BORN I CRIED BUT EVERYONE ELSE REJOICED. WHEN
I DIE EVERYONE ELSE WILL CRY BUT I WILL REJOICE.

—Barbara Young

Hot Holiday Punch

8 cups cranberry juice
1 (12-ounce) can frozen apple juice concentrate
3 to 4 cups water
1/4 cup sugar
6 cinnamon sticks
6 whole cloves
1 teaspoon ground allspice

Combine the cranberry juice, apple juice concentrate, water, sugar, cinnamon sticks, cloves and allspice in a large saucepan. Heat until hot, stirring occasionally. Strain into cups.

Serves 8

FIND THE SEED AT THE BOTTOM OF OUR HEART
AND BRING FORTH A FLOWER.

—*Shigenori Kameoka*

Spiced Tea

2 cups unsweetened instant tea mix
1³/4 cups orange-flavored drink mix
³/4 cup lemonade drink mix
1 cup sugar
2 teaspoons ground cinnamon
2 teaspoons ground cloves

Combine the tea mix, orange-flavored drink mix, lemonade drink mix, sugar, cinnamon and cloves in a bowl. Stir to mix well. Store in an airtight container. Add 3 to 4 tablespoons of the mixture to 1 cup very hot water to serve.

Serves 24 to 30

HE WHO IS FILLED WITH LOVE IS FILLED WITH GOD HIMSELF.

—*St. Augustine of Hippo*

soups and salads

Matty was a four-year-old boy in our HeartPrints program. His diagnosis was osteo-scarcoma. I had taken care of him previously through a home health agency for two years. During that time, he was always afraid of me because he knew me as the nurse who came to give him shots.

After being admitted to Hospice of Acadiana, all that changed. The fear went away, and Matty would sit in my lap, tell me stories about swimming in his pool and riding bikes. And of the pretty lady who came to visit him every evening. "She was beautiful," Matty said. "And very soft."

"Who was that lady?" Matty wanted to know. His family was not particularly religious, but one of Matty's aunts seemed to know the answer. And I felt the answer was clear, as well. The pretty lady was Matty's angel.

Matty subsequently died. Less than a year after his death, Matty's grandmother died also. On the last day before she passed away, she could see Matty and told him, "I'm coming, Matty. Grannie's here to take care of you."

—Debbie Tweedel, R.N.

ARTIST: DAREN TUCKER—"THE MUSICAL ANGEL"
Dedicated to her son Edward W. Wynne III (November 6, 1970-April 20, 2002)
"May flights of angels sing thee to thy rest, sweet Prince."

Daren loves using "light against dark to the extreme." However "extreme," she still describes her work as traditional and reminiscent of her southern French heritage. Her paintings can now be found in private collections throughout the United States.

Crawfish Bisque

1/2 cup vegetable oil
1/2 cup all-purpose flour
1 large onion, chopped
1 rib celery, finely chopped
1 garlic clove, minced
2 quarts boiling water
1 teaspoon salt
1/2 teaspoon cayenne pepper

1/8 teaspoon black pepper
Pinch of sugar
2 pounds crawfish tails in fat, peeled
1/2 cup chopped fresh parsley
4 green onion tops, chopped
Hot steamed rice
Stuffed Crawfish Heads (below)

Heat the oil in a large Dutch oven. Stir in the flour. Cook until dark brown but not burned, stirring constantly. Add the onion, celery and garlic and cook until the onions are tender. Stir in the boiling water slowly. Boil gently for 30 minutes. Stir in the next 4 ingredients. Simmer, covered, for 1 hour. Add the crawfish and cook over medium heat for 15 minutes. Remove from the heat. Stir in the parsley and green onion tops. Ladle over hot rice in bowls. Top with Stuffed Crawfish Heads.

Serves 12

Stuffed Crawfish Heads

4 or 5 slices French bread, toasted
    and torn into pieces
8 ounces crawfish tails, peeled
1/4 cup vegetable oil
1 large onion, finely chopped
2 ribs celery, finely chopped
2 bell peppers, finely chopped

2 garlic cloves, minced
1 tablespoon salt
1/2 teaspoon black pepper
1/2 teaspoon cayenne pepper
4 ounces crawfish tails, peeled
60 crawfish heads, cleaned
Seasoned bread crumbs

Process the toasted bread and 8 ounces crawfish in a food processor until finely chopped. Heat the oil in a large saucepan. Add the onion, celery and bell peppers and sauté until the vegetables are tender. Stir in the bread mixture. Add the garlic, salt, black pepper, cayenne pepper and 4 ounces crawfish. Cook for 5 to 8 minutes, stirring constantly. Remove from the heat and let cool. Pack the mixture tightly into the crawfish heads. Roll the stuffed heads in bread crumbs to coat. Arrange on a large baking pan. Bake at 375 degrees for 15 to 29 minutes.

corn and crab Bisque

1/2 cup (1 stick) butter
1 large onion, chopped
1/2 red bell pepper, chopped
1/2 green bell pepper, chopped
2 ribs celery, chopped
3 garlic cloves, minced
1/3 cup all-purpose flour
1 (10-ounce) can condensed
     cream of shrimp soup
1 cup milk
2 (16-ounce) bags frozen Shoe Peg corn
2 cups (about) half-and-half
1 tablespoon salt
1 teaspoon pepper
1/2 teaspoon thyme (optional)
1/2 cup dry white wine (optional)
1 pound white crab meat, drained and flaked
8 ounces lump crab meat, drained
3 tablespoons chopped green onions
3 tablespoons chopped fresh parsley

Melt the butter in a 4-quart saucepan over low heat. Add the onion, red bell
pepper, green bell pepper, celery and garlic and sauté for 20 minutes over low heat.
Add the flour and cook for a few minutes, stirring constantly. Stir in the shrimp
soup and milk. Combine 1/2 of one bag of corn and 1/2 of the half-and-half in a
blender. Process until mushy. Add to the saucepan. Stir in the remaining corn. Stir
in the remaining half-and-half to desired consistency. Stir in the salt, pepper, thyme,
wine and white crab meat. Cook until heated through. Ladle into serving bowls and
top with the lump crab meat, green onions and parsley.

Serves 10 to 12

world champion chili

2 tablespoons vegetable oil
2¹/2 pounds beef brisket,
    cut into 1-inch cubes
1 pound lean ground pork
1 large onion, finely chopped
Salt and pepper to taste
3 garlic cloves, minced
2 tablespoons chopped green chiles
1 (8-ounce) can tomato sauce
1 beef bouillon cube
1 (12-ounce) can beer
1¹/4 cups water or beer
4 to 6 tablespoons chili powder
2¹/2 tablespoons cumin
¹/8 teaspoon dry mustard
¹/8 teaspoon brown sugar
1 pinch oregano

Heat the oil in a large heavy saucepan. Add the beef, pork and onion and sauté until browned. Season with salt and pepper. Add the garlic, green chiles, tomato sauce, bouillon cube, beer, water, chili powder, cumin, dry mustard, brown sugar and oregano. Stir to mix well. Simmer, covered, for 3 to 4 hours or until the meat is tender and the chili is thick, stirring occasionally.

Serves 4

NOTE: You may have the butcher coarsely grind the beef instead of cutting into 1-inch cubes.

white chili

1 tablespoon vegetable oil
2 onions, chopped (1 cup)
2 garlic cloves, minced
3 cups fat-free chicken broth
2 tablespoons chopped fresh cilantro
2 tablespoons lime juice
1 teaspoon cumin
1/2 teaspoon oregano
1/4 teaspoon hot red pepper sauce
1/4 teaspoon salt
1 (4-ounce) can chopped green chiles
1 (11-ounce) can white Shoe Peg corn or
   whole kernel corn, drained
1 (15- to 16-ounce) can Great Northern
   beans, drained
1 (15- to 16-ounce) can butter beans, drained
2 cups fat-free half-and-half
1 cup water
2 cups chopped cooked chicken breast
1 cup chopped cooked smoked sausage

Heat the oil in a heavy 4-quart Dutch oven over medium heat. Add the onions and garlic and sauté until the onions are tender. Stir in the chicken broth, cilantro, lime juice, cumin, oregano, hot sauce, salt, green chiles, corn, Great Northern beans, butter beans, half-and-half and water. Bring to a boil and reduce the heat. Simmer, uncovered, for 20 minutes. Stir in the chicken and sausage. Cook until heated through.

Serves 6

Hen and Sausage Gumbo

1 (5- to 6-pound) hen or chicken, cut up
2 pounds smoked sausage, sliced
4 quarts water
1 large jar dark roux
3 large onions, finely chopped
1 bell pepper, finely chopped
3 or 4 ribs celery, finely chopped
1 garlic bulb, minced
1 tablespoon salt (or to taste)
1 teaspoon black pepper (or to taste)
1 teaspoon cayenne pepper (or to taste)
10 drops hot red pepper sauce (or to taste)
1 cup finely chopped green onion tops
2 cups finely chopped fresh parsley
Hot cooked rice

Brown the chicken and sausage in a large nonstick stockpot. Remove to a platter. Pour the water into the stockpot and bring to a boil. Add the roux and stir until dissolved. Stir in the onions, bell pepper, celery and garlic. Cook for 15 minutes. Add the chicken and sausage and simmer for about 2 hours. Stir in the salt, black pepper, cayenne and hot sauce. Stir in the green onion tops and parsley. Serve over rice.

Serves 16

Smoked Duck and Andouille Gumbo

1 (4- to 5-pound) duckling
2 cups dark roux
2 onions, chopped
4 ribs celery, chopped
2 bell peppers, chopped
2 tablespoons chopped garlic
2 tablespoons seasoned salt
1 teaspoon white pepper
1 tablespoon Tabasco sauce
1 pound andouille, cut into cubes
1/4 cup chopped green onions
1/4 cup chopped fresh parsley
Hot steamed rice

Smoke the duck. Cut the duck into cubes, reserving the bones for the stock. You may prepare up to this point the day before serving and chill in the refrigerator. Place the reserved bones in a 2-gallon stockpot and cover with water. Simmer for 2 hours. Strain and return the stock to the saucepan, discarding the bones. Bring to a boil and add the roux. Whisk for 15 minutes or until the roux dissolves. Stir in the onions, celery, bell peppers, garlic, seasoned salt, white pepper and Tabasco sauce. Simmer for 1 hour or until the vegetables are tender. Adjust the seasonings to taste. Stir in the duck meat, sausage, green onions and parsley. Simmer for 15 minutes. Serve over rice.

Serves 6 to 8

NOTE: This recipe is donated by Charley G's Seafood Grill.

shrimp and crab Gumbo à la Louie

1/4 cup vegetable oil
1 to 1 1/2 pounds okra, chopped
4 onions, finely chopped
1 1/2 cups finely chopped celery
2 bell peppers, finely chopped
1/4 cup vinegar
1 (10-ounce) can tomatoes with
   green chiles
5 tomatoes, finely chopped or
   1 (15-ounce) can whole tomatoes
4 to 5 cups water or shrimp stock
1 teaspoon basil

1 teaspoon thyme
5 bay leaves
1/4 cup roux (optional)
Browning agent (optional)
Cajun seasoning to taste
Tabasco sauce to taste
1 pound crab meat, drained and flaked
4 to 5 pounds fresh headless shrimp
1 cup finely chopped green onions
1 cup finely chopped fresh parsley
Hot cooked rice

Heat the oil in a very large saucepan. Add the okra and sauté for a few minutes.
Add the onions, celery and bell peppers. Stir in the vinegar, tomatoes with green
chiles and chopped tomatoes. Simmer for 1 to 1 1/2 hours or until the vegetables are
tender. Stir in the water, basil, thyme, bay leaves and roux. Add browning agent if
the color is too light or too red. Season with Cajun seasoning and Tabasco sauce.
Stir in the crab meat and cook for 20 minutes. Stir in the shrimp, green onions and
parsley. Cook for 5 to 10 minutes or until the shrimp turn pink. Discard the bay
leaves and serve the gumbo over rice.

Serves 12 to 15

Sweet Potato and Andouille Soup

3 large sweet potatoes, peeled and chopped
1/2 bunch celery, chopped
2 large onions, chopped
2 quarts chicken stock
2 bay leaves
1 tablespoon basil
1 teaspoon ground cloves (optional)
1/4 teaspoon nutmeg
1/8 teaspoon ground cinnamon
1 tablespoon Worcestershire sauce
1 1/2 to 3 teaspoons Tabasco sauce
1 pound andouille, chopped
1 large onion, finely chopped
2 cups evaporated skim milk
Salt and pepper to taste

Combine the sweet potatoes, celery, 2 chopped onions, the chicken stock, bay leaves, basil, cloves, nutmeg, cinnamon, Worcestershire sauce and Tabasco in a large stockpot. Bring to a boil, stirring occasionally. Reduce the heat. Simmer, uncovered, for 30 minutes. Strain and return the liquid to the stockpot, discarding the solids. Purée the vegetables in a blender or food processor. Add to the stockpot. Sauté the sausage and 1 finely chopped onion in a skillet. Add to the stockpot. Simmer, uncovered, for 15 minutes. Stir in the evaporated milk. Season with salt and pepper. Simmer for 5 minutes.

Serves 8

Taco Soup

1 pound lean ground beef
1 large onion, finely chopped
1 (15-ounce) can pinto beans
1 (15-ounce) can kidney beans
1 (16-ounce) can black-eyed peas with jalapeños
1 (14-ounce) can chopped tomatoes or
  1 (10-ounce) can tomatoes with green chiles
1 (4-ounce) can chopped green chiles
1 (15-ounce) can whole kernel corn
1 can tomato sauce
1¹/₂ cups water
1 package taco seasoning mix
1 package ranch salad dressing mix

Brown the ground beef in a skillet with the onion, stirring until the ground beef is crumbly; drain. Remove to a stockpot. Cook until hot. Stir in the pinto beans, kidney beans, black-eyed peas, tomatoes, green chiles, corn, tomato sauce, water, taco seasoning and salad dressing mix. Bring to a boil and reduce the heat. Simmer for at least 20 to 30 minutes, stirring occasionally.

Serves 4 to 6

NOTE: This soup freezes well and tastes even better when reheated.

chicken and squash soup

2 to 4 tablespoons vegetable oil
5 boneless skinless chicken breasts
1 cup (2 sticks) butter
4 small yellow squash, cubed
4 small zucchini, cubed
2 bell peppers, chopped
2 onions, chopped
2 potatoes, cubed
2 tablespoons Cajun seasoning
1 teaspoon garlic salt
1/2 teaspoon black pepper
1/2 teaspoon cayenne pepper
1/4 cup all-purpose flour
5 cups hot water
1/4 block (2 to 3 inches) Velveeta cheese, cubed
3 cups half-and-half

Heat the oil in a heavy stockpot. Add the chicken and cook until browned. Remove the chicken and cut into cubes. Add the butter to the saucepan and heat until melted. Add the yellow squash, zucchini, bell peppers, onions, potatoes, Cajun seasoning, garlic salt, black pepper and cayenne pepper. Sauté for 30 minutes or until the squash is tender. Stir in a mixture of the flour and water. Add the chicken and reduce the heat to medium. Simmer for 30 minutes. Reduce the heat to low and stir in the cheese and half-and-half. Cook until the cheese melts, stirring constantly. Do not let boil.

Serves 8

corn and shrimp soup

1/2 cup (1 stick) margarine
3/4 cup chopped onion
1/2 cup chopped celery
1/4 cup chopped bell pepper
1/3 cup all-purpose flour
1 pound fresh shrimp
2 (10-ounce) cans chicken broth
1 (10-ounce) can evaporated milk
2 (14-ounce) cans whole kernel corn, drained
1 (14-ounce) can cream-style corn
Garlic powder to taste
Cayenne pepper to taste

Melt the margarine in a large saucepan. Add the onion, celery and bell pepper and sauté until the vegetables are tender. Reduce the heat to low and stir in the flour. Cook for a few minutes or until smooth, stirring constantly; do not brown. Add the shrimp and cook until the shrimp turn pink. Stir in the chicken broth and evaporated milk. Cook until thickened, stirring often. Stir in the whole kernel corn and cream-style corn. Season with garlic powder and cayenne pepper. Cook until heated through. Ladle into serving bowls or bread bowls.

Serves 8

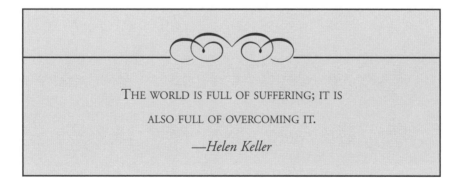

THE WORLD IS FULL OF SUFFERING; IT IS

ALSO FULL OF OVERCOMING IT.

—*Helen Keller*

Asparagus Soup

2 pounds asparagus
1/4 cup (1/2 stick) butter
1 1/2 cups sliced leeks
3 tablespoons all-purpose flour
6 cups chicken broth
1 egg yolk
2 tablespoons butter (optional)
Salt and freshly ground pepper to taste

Cut off the top 3 inches of the asparagus. Blanch the tips in a saucepan of boiling water for 3 to 5 minutes; drain. Cool and chop. Trim the remaining asparagus spears and cut into 1/2-inch pieces. Melt 1/4 cup butter in a large saucepan over low heat. Add the leeks and sauté until tender but not browned. Stir in the uncooked asparagus pieces. Cook, covered, for 5 to 10 minutes. Stir in the flour. Cook for 2 to 3 minutes, stirring constantly. Stir in the broth and bring to a boil. Reduce the heat and partially cover. Simmer for 30 minutes. Purée the soup in batches in a blender or food processor. Strain the puréed soup through a sieve to remove any fibers. Add 1/2 the cooked asparagus tips and process until finely chopped. Return to the saucepan. Beat the egg yolk in a small bowl. Whisk in 1/2 cup of the hot soup. Whisk back into the soup in the saucepan. Stir in the remaining chopped asparagus tips and 2 tablespoons butter. Cook until heated through; do not boil. Season with salt and pepper.

Serves 6 to 8

Black Bean Soup

4 cups dried black beans	1/2 cup (1 stick) butter
5 quarts water	3 large onions, finely chopped
1 smoked rind-on ham bone	3 ribs celery, finely chopped
3 bunches green onions, chopped	2 1/2 tablespoons all-purpose flour
4 bay leaves	1/2 cup finely chopped fresh parsley
1 tablespoon salt	1 (10-ounce) can beef consommé
1/2 teaspoon pepper	(optional)
2 garlic cloves	1 cup madeira (or to taste)

Cover the beans with water in a large saucepan and let soak overnight. Rinse and drain the beans. Return the beans to the saucepan. Add 5 quarts water, the ham bone, green onions, bay leaves, salt, pepper and garlic. Bring to a boil and reduce the heat to a simmer. Melt the butter in a skillet. Add the onions and celery and sauté until the vegetables are tender. Stir in the flour and parsley. Cook for a few minutes or until smooth, stirring constantly. Stir into the bean mixture. Simmer for at least 6 hours. Add boiling water if needed to keep the beans covered. Remove and discard the ham bone and bay leaves. Purée the soup in a blender. Pour through a fine mesh strainer back into the saucepan. Taste and adjust the seasonings. Stir in the consommé if a richer taste is desired. Cook the soup until heated through. Stir in the madeira. Serve garnished with lemon slices and parsley.

Serves 12

NOTE: This soup can be frozen before adding the madeira. Do not substitute sherry for madeira.

white Bean Soup

1 pound dried white beans
2 cups chopped honey ham
2 onions, chopped
Salt and pepper to taste
Olive oil
1/4 cup minced garlic
4 ribs celery, chopped
1 large onion, chopped
2 (14-ounce) cans stewed tomatoes
1/8 to 1/4 cup chopped fresh basil
2 cans white Shoe Peg corn or cream-style corn
Chicken stock (optional)

Cover the beans with water in a large saucepan and let soak overnight. Rinse and drain the beans. Return the beans to the saucepan and cover with water. Bring to a boil. Boil for 20 minutes. Drain and return the beans to the saucepan. Add water to cover the beans by 2 inches. Add the ham and 2 onions. Season with salt and pepper. Simmer for 2 hours or until the beans are almost tender. Heat a small amount of olive oil in a large skillet. Add the garlic, celery and 1 onion and sauté until the vegetables are tender. Stir in the tomatoes, basil and corn. Cook for 10 to 20 minutes, stirring occasionally. Stir into the bean mixture. Stir in chicken stock. Cook until heated through.

Serves 15

Beer Cheese Soup

1/4 cup (1/2 stick) butter or margarine
1/4 cup all-purpose flour
1/2 cup grated carrots
1/2 cup finely chopped onion
2 1/2 cups milk
1 (15-ounce) jar Cheez Whiz
1 teaspoon caraway seeds
Salt and pepper to taste
6 to 12 ounces beer, at room temperature
Finely chopped fresh parsley

Melt the butter in a saucepan over low heat. Stir in the flour. Cook for a few minutes, stirring constantly. Add the carrots and onion and sauté until the vegetables are tender. Stir in the milk gradually. Cook until thickened, stirring constantly. Stir in the Cheez Whiz and caraway seeds. Season with salt and pepper. Stir in the beer slowly. Cook just until heated through. Ladle into serving bowls or bread bowls and top each with a pinch of parsley.

Serves 4 to 6

IF YOU THINK BACK, YOU WILL SEE YOUR WHOLE LIFE IS A STORY OF
GOD'S LOVE COMING UPON YOU IN SUCCESSIVE STAGES.

—Pope John Paul II

Broccoli Cheese Soup

2 tablespoons butter
1 cup chopped onion
2 garlic cloves, minced
3 cups chicken broth
1 (16-ounce) package frozen
  chopped broccoli, thawed
2¹/2 cups milk
¹/3 cup all-purpose flour
¹/4 teaspoon pepper
8 ounces Velveeta cheese, cubed

Melt the butter in a large saucepan. Add the onion and garlic and sauté until the onion is tender. Stir in the chicken broth and broccoli. Cook over medium-high heat for 10 minutes, stirring occasionally. Mix the milk and flour in a bowl. Stir gradually into the broccoli mixture. Cook for 10 minutes or until slightly thickened, stirring constantly. Stir in the pepper. Remove from the heat and add the cheese. Stir until the cheese melts. Remove ¹/3 of the mixture to a blender and purée. Return to the saucepan and stir to blend.

Serves 6

corn chowder

6 slices bacon
1 onion, chopped
2 potatoes, peeled, cooked and diced
$1/2$ cup water
2 cups milk
1 (14-ounce) can cream-style corn
$1/2$ teaspoon salt
Dash of pepper

Cook the bacon in a large saucepan until crisp. Remove to paper towels to drain; crumble. Remove all but 2 tablespoons of bacon drippings from the saucepan. Add the onion and sauté until tender. Stir in the potatoes and water. Cover and let simmer. Stir in the milk, corn, salt and pepper. Cook over medium heat until hot, stirring often. Ladle into serving bowls and sprinkle with the crumbled bacon.

Serves 5

THERE IS NO CHARITY WITHOUT PATIENCE. NEITHER
IS THERE PATIENCE WITHOUT CHARITY.

—*St. Catherine of Sienna*

Cream of Potato Soup

1/4 to 1/2 cup (1/2 to 1 stick) margarine
1 large bag frozen hash brown potatoes
1 large onion, finely chopped
1/2 teaspoon rosemary, crushed
3 (14-ounce) cans chicken broth
2 cups half-and-half
1/4 cup all-purpose flour
1 (10-ounce) can condensed
   Cheddar cheese soup
Crumbled cooked bacon or
   chopped ham (optional)
Salt and pepper to taste

Melt the margarine in a large saucepan. Add the potatoes and sauté until tender. Add the onion and rosemary. Sauté until the onion is tender and the potatoes are beginning to brown. Stir in the chicken broth. Bring to a boil over medium-high heat. Reduce the heat and simmer for 30 minutes. Mix the half-and-half and flour in a bowl. Stir into the potato mixture. Simmer until thickened, stirring constantly. Stir in the cheese soup and bacon. Cook until heated through. Season with salt and pepper.

Serves 6 to 8

NOTE: This soup can be frozen for up to 2 months.

Cream of Tomato Basil Soup

1 (46-ounce) can tomato juice
1 (46-ounce) can vegetable juice cocktail
2 large garlic cloves, minced
1/2 teaspoon coarsely ground pepper
1 teaspoon basil
2 cups heavy cream
1 cup half-and-half

Combine the tomato juice and vegetable juice cocktail in a large saucepan. Bring to a slow boil. Stir in the garlic, pepper and basil and reduce the heat. Simmer until the mixture is reduced by 1/3. Stir in the cream and half-and-half. Remove from the heat and cover. Let stand for 15 minutes.

Serves 10 to 12

ENTRUST THE PAST TO GOD'S MERCY, THE PRESENT TO
HIS LOVE, AND THE FUTURE TO HIS PROVIDENCE.

—St. Augustine of Hippo

Hot Chicken Salad

1/2 cup slivered almonds
2 cups cubed cooked rotisserie chicken
1 (8-ounce) can sliced water chestnuts, drained
1 (4-ounce) jar diced pimentos, drained
1/4 teaspoon salt
1/4 teaspoon pepper
1/4 teaspoon celery salt
1/4 teaspoon MSG
2 tablespoons lemon juice
1 cup mayonnaise
1 (2-ounce) can French-fried onions

Spread the almonds on a baking sheet. Bake at 300 degrees for 20 to 30 minutes or until lightly browned, stirring occasionally. Remove to a large bowl. Add the chicken, water chestnuts, pimentos, salt, pepper, celery salt, MSG, lemon juice and mayonnaise. Stir to mix well. Spoon into a 9×13-inch baking dish coated with nonstick cooking spray. Sprinkle with the French-fried onions. Bake at 350 degrees for 30 minutes.

Serves 8 to 10

Shrimp Rémoulade

1 cup mayonnaise
1 cup Zataran's Creole mustard
2 garlic cloves, minced
Juice of 1 lemon
1 bunch celery, chopped
¹/4 cup chopped green onion tops
1 tablespoon chopped fresh parsley
Grated fresh horseradish to taste
5 pounds peeled cooked shrimp
Shredded lettuce

Combine the mayonnaise, Creole mustard, garlic, lemon juice, celery, green onion tops and parsley in a large bowl. Stir to mix well. Season with horseradish. Stir in the shrimp. Cover and chill. Serve over shredded lettuce.

Serves 8

STRENGTH AND COURAGE AREN'T ALWAYS MEASURED IN MEDALS AND VICTORIES. THEY ARE MEASURED IN THE STRUGGLES THEY OVERCOME. THE STRONGEST PEOPLE AREN'T ALWAYS THE PEOPLE WHO WIN, BUT THE PEOPLE WHO DON'T GIVE UP WHEN THEY LOSE.

—*Ashley Hodgeson*

Greek Pasta Salad

1/2 cup mayonnaise
1/2 cup olive oil
4 1/2 tablespoons Cavender's Greek seasoning
4 1/2 tablespoons fresh lemon juice
1 bunch green onions, chopped
1 (4-ounce) jar diced pimentos, drained
1 (4-ounce) can chopped
  black olives, drained
12 to 16 ounces angel hair pasta,
  broken into thirds

Combine the mayonnaise, olive oil, Greek seasoning and lemon juice in a large bowl. Stir to mix well. Stir in the green onions, pimentos and olives. Cook the pasta in a large saucepan of boiling water until al dente; drain well. Add the warm pasta to the mayonnaise mixture and toss to mix.

Serves 4 to 6

LET US BE GRATEFUL TO PEOPLE WHO MAKE US HAPPY, THEY ARE THE

CHARMING GARDENERS WHO MAKE OUR SOULS BLOSSOM.

—*Marcel Proust*

Marinated Green Bean Salad

5 (14-ounce) cans whole green beans
2 (14-ounce) cans quartered artichoke hearts
1 (8-ounce) can sliced water chestnuts, drained
1 cup vegetable oil
1 cup sugar
1/2 cup red wine vinegar
1 tablespoon soy sauce
Salt and pepper to taste
1/4 cup (1/2 stick) butter
1 (3-ounce) package ramen noodles
1 cup walnuts or pecans, chopped

Drain the beans, artichokes and water chestnuts into a colander. Combine the oil, sugar, vinegar and soy sauce in a jar with a tight-fitting lid. Season with salt and pepper. Shake to mix well. Combine the drained vegetables and oil mixture in a large sealable plastic bag. Seal the bag and chill overnight. Melt the butter in a skillet. Crush the ramen noodles in the package. Discard the seasoning packet and add the crushed noodles and walnuts to the skillet. Sauté until golden brown. Remove from the heat and let cool. Pour the vegetable mixture into a colander and drain well. Remove to a large bowl. Add the noodle mixture and toss to mix.

Serves 8 to 10

Nutty Broccoli Salad

1 small package slivered almonds
1 cup mayonnaise
1/4 cup sugar
1 to 2 tablespoons cider vinegar
1 bunch broccoli florets, cut into bite-size pieces
1/2 cup chopped celery
1/4 cup chopped green onions
1 cup halved red grapes
8 ounces bacon, crisp-cooked and crumbled

Spread the almonds on a baking sheet. Bake at 350 degrees for 5 to 7 minutes or until lightly toasted, stirring occasionally. Whisk the mayonnaise, sugar and vinegar together in a small bowl and set aside. Combine the broccoli, celery, green onions and grapes in a large bowl and mix well. Add the toasted almonds, bacon and mayonnaise mixture just before serving and toss to mix.

Serves 4

Crunchy Coleslaw

2 (3-ounce) packages oriental-flavor
  ramen noodles
3/4 cup vegetable oil
1/4 cup white vinegar
3 tablespoons sugar
2 ounces toasted slivered almonds
4 ounces roasted unsalted sunflower seeds
1 (16-ounce) package coleslaw mix

Whisk the seasoning packets from the ramen noodles, the oil, vinegar, sugar, almonds and sunflower seeds in a bowl. Crush the ramen noodles into a large bowl. Add the coleslaw mix and toss to combine. Pour the dressing over the coleslaw mixture just before serving and toss to mix.

Serves 8

Sour Cream Cucumber Salad

1/2 cup white vinegar
1/2 cup water
1 tablespoon sugar
1/2 teaspoon salt
2 cucumbers, peeled and cut into 1/8-inch slices
1/2 cup sour cream
1/8 teaspoon white pepper
1 tablespoon chopped fresh parsley

Mix the vinegar, water, sugar and salt together in a glass or plastic bowl. Add the cucumbers and stir to mix. Cover and chill for 2 to 24 hours. Drain well and return to the bowl. Stir in the sour cream and pepper. Sprinkle with the parsley and serve immediately.

Serves 4

Christmas Potato Salad

6 hard-cooked eggs, chilled
Mayonnaise to taste
12 Irish potatoes, peeled, cooked,
*   cubed and chilled*
3 ribs celery, chopped and chilled
4 tomatoes, chopped and chilled
1 large green bell pepper, chopped and chilled

Cut the eggs in half and remove the yolks to a small bowl. Mash and stir in mayonnaise until smooth. Chop the egg whites finely. Combine the potatoes, celery, tomatoes, bell pepper, egg yolks and egg whites in a large bowl. Stir in mayonnaise to desired consistency. Serve cold.

Serves 15

Autumn Dinner Salad

2 tablespoons butter
3 tablespoons brown sugar
1/2 cup chopped pecans
Mixed salad greens
1 pear or apple, cored and sliced
4 ounces Gorgonzola or blue cheese, crumbled
Dressing (below)

Melt the butter in a skillet. Stir in the brown sugar. Add the pecans and sauté until softened. Remove from the heat and let cool. Combine the salad greens, pear, cheese and pecans in a large bowl. Toss to mix. Add the Dressing and toss to coat.

Serves 4

Dressing

1/2 cup olive oil
1/4 cup balsamic vinegar
3 garlic cloves, minced
1/2 teaspoon salt
1/4 teaspoon pepper

Whisk the olive oil, vinegar, garlic, salt and pepper in a bowl.

Layered Salad

1 head romaine, chopped
1 red onion, chopped
1 bunch celery, chopped
1 bell pepper, chopped
1 (10-ounce) package frozen
    green peas, thawed

2 cups mayonnaise
Grated Romano cheese
3 or 4 slices bacon, crisp-cooked
    and crumbled

Spread the romaine in a 9×13-inch baking dish or large bowl. Sprinkle with the onion, celery, bell pepper and peas in the order listed. Spread the mayonnaise over the top and sprinkle with cheese and the bacon. Cover and chill overnight.

Serves 8 to 10

Fresh Spinach Salad with Orange Curry Dressing

1 cup cider vinegar
1/2 cup sugar
2 heaping tablespoons orange
    marmalade
2 teaspoons curry powder
2 teaspoons dry mustard
2 teaspoons salt
1 teaspoon freshly ground pepper
1/2 teaspoon Tabasco sauce

1 3/4 cups vegetable oil
4 bunches fresh spinach, trimmed
5 Red Delicious apples, chopped
2 cups golden raisins
1 3/4 cups walnut halves
6 green onions, chopped
1/4 cup sesame seeds, toasted
1 pound bacon, crisp-cooked and
    crumbled

Process the vinegar, sugar, marmalade, curry powder, dry mustard, salt, pepper and Tabasco sauce in a blender or food processor. Add the oil in a fine stream, processing constantly at high speed until thickened. Let stand at room temperature for 2 hours. Cover and chill. Divide the spinach among 12 salad plates. Drizzle with the dressing. Top each serving evenly with apples, raisins, walnuts, green onions, sesame seeds and bacon.

Serves 12

Orange and Avocado Spinach Salad

8 to 12 ounces baby spinach, trimmed and washed
3 tablespoons fresh lemon juice
$^1/_2$ to 1 teaspoon salt
$^1/_4$ cup honey
Pepper to taste
$^1/_2$ cup mild extra-virgin olive oil
2 tablespoons finely chopped red onion
1$^1/_2$ teaspoons finely chopped fresh mint or
   1 teaspoon crushed dried mint
4 or 5 seedless oranges
2 or 3 ripe avocados

Wrap the spinach in a damp kitchen towel. Chill for at least 2 hours to crisp. Stir the lemon juice and salt in a bowl until the salt dissolves. Whisk in the honey. Season with pepper. Whisk in the olive oil, onion and mint. Taste and adjust the seasonings. Peel the oranges and remove any white pith. Cut crosswise into thin slices. Peel and pit the avocados. Cut lengthwise into thin slices. Arrange the spinach on salad plates. Top with the avocado slices and orange slices. Whisk the dressing and drizzle over the salad.

Serves 8

WE CAN NEVER OBTAIN PEACE IN THE OUTER WORLD

UNTIL WE MAKE PEACE WITH OURSELVES.

—*Dalai Lama*

Spinach and Pear Salad

4 firm ripe pears
1/3 cup fresh lime juice
1 teaspoon grated lime zest
1/3 cup honey
3 tablespoons olive oil
1/8 teaspoon pepper
4 cups torn fresh spinach
3/4 cup torn radicchio
1/2 cup coarsely chopped walnuts
4 ounces feta cheese, crumbled

Core the pears and cut each lengthwise into 8 wedges. Toss the pears with
1 tablespoon of the lime juice in a bowl. Combine the lime zest, remaining lime
juice, honey, olive oil and and pepper in a jar with a tight-fitting lid. Shake to mix
well. Arrange the spinach and radicchio on 8 salad plates. Fan 4 pear wedges on
top of each. Sprinkle with the walnuts and cheese. Spoon the dressing over
the salad.

Serves 8

THE PESSIMIST SEES DIFFICULTY IN EVERY OPPORTUNITY.

THE OPTIMIST SEES THE OPPORTUNITY IN EVERY DIFFICULTY.

—Winston Churchill

Merry Cranberry Freeze

1 (12-ounce) bag fresh cranberries, finely chopped
1/2 cup sugar
8 ounces regular or low-fat cream cheese, softened
1 (8-ounce) can crushed pineapple, drained
1/2 cup pecans, chopped
1 (8-ounce) container regular or fat-free frozen
   whipped topping, thawed

Combine the cranberries and sugar in a large bowl. Stir until the sugar dissolves.
Stir in the cream cheese, pineapple and pecans. Fold in the whipped topping.
Spoon into foil-lined muffin cups. Freeze until firm.

Serves 12

Grape Salad

8 ounces cream cheese, softened
3/4 cup sugar
1 cup sour cream
1 teaspoon vanilla extract
1 cup pecans
3 to 4 pounds seedless red or green grapes
Brown sugar

Combine the cream cheese, sugar, sour cream and vanilla in a large bowl. Stir to
mix well. Add the pecans and grapes and toss gently to mix. Spoon into a serving
dish and sprinkle with brown sugar.

Serves 8 to 10

Paper Cup Frozen Fruit Salad

2 cups sour cream
2 tablespoons lemon juice
1/2 cup sugar
Dash of salt
1 (8-ounce) can crushed pineapple, well drained
1 banana, chopped
4 drops red food color
1/4 cup chopped pecans
1 (16-ounce) can Bing cherries, well drained

Mix the sour cream and lemon juice in a large bowl. Stir in the sugar and salt. Stir in the pineapple and banana. Stir in the food color and pecans. Fold in the cherries. Spoon into paper cups and place in muffin cups. Freeze until firm. Remove from the muffin cups and cover each with plastic wrap. Seal in a plastic freezer bag and store in the freezer. Let stand at room temperature for 15 minutes before serving. Peel off the paper cups and place on lettuce leaves.

Serves 12

BEFORE ALL THINGS AND ABOVE ALL THINGS CARE
MUST BE TAKEN OF THE SICK. THEY MUST BE SERVED IN EVERY
DEED AS CHRIST HIMSELF.

—*St. Benedict*

Roquefort Cheese Dressing

8 ounces cream cheese, softened
1 cup sour cream
1 garlic clove, minced
1/4 cup half-and-half
4 1/2 teaspoons white wine vinegar
1/4 teaspoon salt
4 ounces blue cheese, crumbled
4 ounces Roquefort cheese, crumbled

Beat the cream cheese, sour cream, garlic, half-and-half, vinegar and salt in a bowl with an electric mixer. Stir in the blue cheese and Roquefort cheese. Use as a salad dressing or dip.

Serves 12 to 16

Cajun Vinaigrette

1/2 cup rice wine vinegar
2 tablespoons olive oil
2 tablespoons Creole mustard
1 tablespoon chopped fresh basil
Salt and pepper to taste

Whisk the vinegar, olive oil, Creole mustard and basil together in a bowl. Season with salt and pepper. Drizzle over sliced fresh tomato, sliced purple onion and sliced avocado.

Serves 6 to 8

vegetables and sides

Mr. B. and his wife lived outside of St. Martinville in a beautiful log cabin, surrounded by fields and woods. Their children were grown and had moved away, but visited often and enjoyed reminiscing about their childhood. Mr. B. loved rabbits and would not allow the children to shoot them in any way. The night Mr. B. was dying, all the children were home to be with him in his last hours. One of his sons went outside to grieve and was standing near the window of his father's bedroom. A small bunny was at the window and would not move, in spite of the son's efforts to frighten him away. Mr. B. died a short time later. The nurse visited, and the funeral home was called. When the funeral home attendants arrived, the family followed them and Mr. B.'s body out to the hearse to say good-bye. As they turned to go back inside the house, they were amazed to see hundreds of rabbits gathered in the yard. They felt that it was a sign from Mr. B. He was okay, and now they were too.

—Marilyn Arton, R.N., CHPN

ARTIST: PAUL SCHEXNAYDER—"HOUSE OF HOPE"
Submitted in memory of his father, Gordon Allen Schexnayder

Much of his imagery is firmly rooted in the Acadiana folklore of his early years growing up in New Iberia, Louisiana, where he was born. His metaphors find their sources in the universal language of nature, architecture, food, and music that move in and around each painting. His art is shown worldwide and is represented in galleries in Louisiana and Texas.

Broccoli Cheese Casserole

1/2 cup (1 stick) butter
1 onion, chopped
1 rib celery, chopped
1 teaspoon minced garlic
1 can sliced mushrooms, drained
1 (10-ounce) package frozen chopped broccoli,
    cooked and drained
1 (10-ounce) can condensed
    cream of mushroom soup
1 cup chopped Velveeta cheese, or
    1 cup jalapeño Cheez Whiz
1 1/2 cups cooked rice
Tabasco sauce to taste
Creole seasoning to taste
Bread crumbs or 1 (2-ounce) can
    French-fried onions

Melt the butter in a large skillet. Add the onion, celery, garlic and mushrooms and sauté until the vegetables are tender. Remove from the heat. Combine the broccoli, soup and cheese in a large bowl. Stir to mix well. Add the onion mixture. Stir to mix well. Add the rice and season with Tabasco sauce and Creole seasoning. Stir to mix well. Spoon into a greased 9×11-inch casserole. Top with bread crumbs. Bake at 350 degrees for 35 to 45 minutes or until bubbly.

Serves 8 to 10

Cauliflower Au Gratin

1 head cauliflower
1 cup (2 sticks) butter
3/4 cup all-purpose flour
2 cups evaporated milk
2 cups water
1 teaspoon Worcestershire sauce
Salt to taste
16 ounces sharp Cheddar cheese, shredded

Rinse the cauliflower and remove the green stems. Cut into bite-size pieces. Cook in a large saucepan of boiling salted water for 15 minutes or until tender-crisp; drain. Place in a baking dish coated with nonstick cooking spray. Melt the butter in a saucepan. Stir in the flour. Cook for a few minutes, stirring constantly. Do not brown. Mix the evaporated milk and water in a bowl. Stir into the flour mixture gradually. Cook for 10 minutes or until thickened, stirring constantly. Stir in the Worcestershire sauce and season with salt. Pour the white sauce over the cauliflower and cover with the cheese. Bake at 350 degrees for 20 to 25 minutes or until bubbly.

Serves 8

NOTE: This recipe can be used to make Potatoes Au Gratin. Bake longer for the potatoes to become tender.

corn casserole

1/2 cup (1 stick) butter or margarine, melted
1 cup sour cream
1 (15-ounce) can whole kernel corn, drained
1 (14-ounce) can cream-style corn
1 (8-ounce) package corn bread mix
1 1/2 cups (6 ounces) shredded Cheddar cheese

Melt the butter and sour cream in a saucepan over low heat. Remove from the heat and add the whole-kernel corn, cream-style corn and corn bread mix. Stir to mix well. Pour into a casserole dish. Bake at 350 degrees for 20 minutes. Sprinkle with the cheese and bake for 30 to 35 minutes longer.

Serves 8

IF YOU LIVE FOR THE NEXT WORLD, YOU GET THIS
ONE IN THE DEAL; BUT IF YOU LIVE ONLY FOR THIS WORLD,
YOU LOSE THEM BOTH.

—C. S. Lewis

Maque Choux

6 ears fresh corn
2 tablespoons butter
2 onions, chopped
2 bell peppers, chopped
2 garlic cloves, minced
4 fresh tomatoes, chopped
Salt and cayenne pepper to taste
2 tablespoons milk (optional)

Cut the kernels from the cob into a bowl using a sharp knife. Scrape the pulp from the cobs into the bowl. Melt the butter in a skillet. Add the onions, bell peppers and garlic and sauté for 5 minutes. Stir in the tomatoes and corn. Season with salt and cayenne. Simmer, uncovered, for 45 minutes, stirring occasionally. Stir in the milk if the mixture becomes too dry or begins to stick to the skillet.

Serves 8

ANXIOUS HEARTS ARE VERY HEAVY, BUT A WORD OF

ENCOURAGEMENT DOES WONDERS.

—*Proverbs 12:25*

Green Bean Bundles

3 (14-ounce) cans whole green beans
1 pound bacon
1/2 cup (1 stick) butter, melted
1 cup packed brown sugar
1 tablespoon Kikkoman marinade
1/2 teaspoon garlic powder

Drain the beans and reserve the liquid. Cut the bacon slices in half. Wrap 8 to
10 beans in 1/2 slice of bacon and secure with a wooden pick. Repeat to use all the
beans and bacon. Arrange the bean bundles in a single layer in a shallow baking
dish. Whisk the reserved bean liquid, melted butter, brown sugar, marinade and
garlic powder in a bowl. Pour over the bean bundles. Cover and chill overnight.
Remove the bundles from the marinade and discard the marinade. Arrange the
bundles in a single layer on a foil-lined baking sheet. Bake at 350 degrees for
30 to 40 minutes or until browned and crunchy.

Serves 6 to 8

AND HE WILL RAISE YOU UP ON EAGLE'S WINGS, BEAR

YOU ON THE BREATH OF DAWN, MAKE YOU TO SHINE LIKE THE

SUN, AND HOLD YOU IN THE PALM OF HIS HAND.

—From "On Eagle's Wings"

Green Beans Amandine

1 quart fresh green beans, trimmed
1/3 cup olive oil
1/2 cup chopped onion
1/2 cup chopped bell pepper
1/2 cup chopped celery
1/3 cup chopped shallots
1 tablespoon chopped garlic
2 (10-ounce) cans condensed
  cream of mushroom soup
1 teaspoon salt
1 teaspoon cayenne pepper
1 cup sliced almonds
1 1/2 to 2 cups (6 to 8 ounces) shredded Pepper Jack cheese

Cook the beans in a saucepan of boiling water until tender-crisp; drain. Heat the olive oil in a large saucepan. Add the onion, bell pepper, celery, shallots and garlic and sauté until the vegetables are tender. Remove from the heat and stir in the beans. Add the soup, salt and cayenne pepper and stir to mix well. Spoon into a 9×13-inch baking dish. Sprinkle with the almonds and cover the top with the cheese. Bake at 375 degrees for 35 to 40 minutes.

Serves 8

Green Bean Casserole

1/2 to 1 pound bacon
1 onion, chopped
1 (10-ounce) can condensed
*   cream of mushroom soup*
1 (6-ounce) roll garlic cheese or
*   6 ounces Velveeta cheese, cubed*
3 cans cut Blue Lake green beans, drained

Cook the bacon in a large skillet until crisp. Remove to paper towels to drain;
crumble. Remove all but 2 tablespoons of the bacon drippings from the saucepan.
Add the onion and sauté until tender. Stir in the soup and cheese. Cook over low
heat until the cheese melts, stirring often. Place the beans in a casserole. Add the
cheese mixture. Stir gently to mix. Sprinkle with the bacon. Bake at 375 degrees
for 30 minutes.

Serves 6

EVERY TOMORROW HAS TWO HANDLES. WE CAN TAKE HOLD OF IT

BY THE HANDLE OF ANXIETY, OR BY THE HANDLE OF FAITH.

—Author Unknown

Eggplant Casserole

2 eggplant, peeled and cubed
2 tablespoons butter
1 cup chopped onion
1 cup chopped celery
1 cup chopped bell pepper
2 garlic cloves, minced
1 pound lean ground beef, peeled shrimp
   or crab meat
Seasoned bread crumbs
2 tablespoons butter, cut up

Cook the eggplant in a saucepan of boiling water until tender; drain. Melt
2 tablespoons butter in a large saucepan. Add the onion, celery, bell pepper and
garlic and sauté until the vegetables are tender. Add the ground beef and cook,
stirring until the meat is crumbly and cooked through; drain. Stir in the eggplant.
Spoon into a buttered casserole. Top with bread crumbs and dot with 2 tablespoons
butter. Bake at 350 degrees for 30 minutes.

Serves 6

Eggplant Stacks

1 large eggplant, peeled and cut into $^1/_2$-inch slices
2 large tomatoes, sliced
1 large onion, thinly sliced
$^1/_4$ cup olive oil
$^1/_2$ to 1 teaspoon salt
10 fresh basil leaves
4 ounces provolone cheese, sliced
$^1/_2$ cup Italian-style seasoned bread crumbs

Arrange the eggplant slices on a nonstick baking sheet. Top each with a slice of tomato and a slice of onion. Drizzle with the olive oil. Sprinkle with the salt and top each with a basil leaf. Cover with foil. Bake at 350 degrees for 30 minutes. Remove the foil and top each stack with a slice of cheese and sprinkle with the bread crumbs. Bake at 450 degrees for 10 minutes. Serve hot or cold.

Serves 10

WE CAN DO NO GREAT THINGS, ONLY SMALL

THINGS WITH GREAT LOVE.

—Mother Theresa of Calcutta

Smothered Mustard Greens

2 bunches mustard greens
1/4 cup olive oil
1/2 cup chopped onion
1/2 cup chopped bell pepper
1/3 cup chopped shallots
1 tablespoon chopped garlic
1/2 cup chopped tasso
1/2 cup chopped smoked pork sausage
1 tablespoon cayenne pepper
1 teaspoon salt
1 teaspoon sugar or equivalent sugar substitute
1/4 teaspoon oregano
1/4 teaspoon thyme
1 1/2 cups water
1/4 cup red wine vinegar (optional)
1/4 cup olive oil (optional)

Wash the mustard greens and remove the ribs. Chop into bite-size pieces. Heat 1/4 cup olive oil in a large saucepan. Add the onion, bell pepper, shallots and garlic and sauté until the vegetables are tender. Remove the sautéed vegetables to a large saucepan or stockpot. Stir in the tasso, smoked sausage, cayenne pepper, salt, sugar, oregano, thyme, water and mustard greens. Cook until the mustard greens are dark green and wilted, stirring often. Remove from the heat and stir in the vinegar and 1/4 cup olive oil or add the vinegar and olive oil to individual servings.

Serves 6

French Onion Casserole

3 sweet onions
2 tablespoons butter
8 ounces fresh mushrooms, sliced
1 cup (4 ounces) shredded Swiss cheese
1 (10-ounce) can condensed
  cream of mushroom soup
1 (5-ounce) can evaporated milk
2 teaspoons soy sauce
6 (1/2-inch) slices French bread
1 cup (4 ounces) shredded Swiss cheese
1/4 cup finely chopped fresh parsley

Slice the onions crosswise through the center and cut each section in half. Melt the butter in a large skillet over medium-high heat. Add the onions and mushrooms and sauté until the vegetables are tender. Spoon into a lightly greased 2-quart baking dish. Sprinkle with 1 cup cheese. Combine the soup, evaporated milk and soy sauce in a bowl. Stir to mix well. Pour over the onion mixture. Arrange the bread slices on top. Sprinkle with 1 cup cheese and the parsley. Cover and chill for 4 to 8 hours. Let stand at room temperature for 30 minutes. Bake, covered, at 375 degrees for 30 minutes. Uncover and bake for 15 to 20 minutes longer or until heated through. Let stand for 5 minutes before serving.

Serves 6 to 8

Sweet Onion and Potato Gratin

1/2 cup (1 stick) butter
3 tablespoons all-purpose flour
2 cups heavy cream
3 ounces shredded Cheddar cheese
Salt and pepper to taste
2 1/2 pounds sliced peeled potatoes
2 1/2 cups sliced sweet onions
6 ounces provolone cheese, sliced
1/3 cup chopped fresh parsley

Melt the butter in a saucepan. Whisk in the flour. Cook for a few minutes, whisking constantly. Whisk in the cream and Cheddar cheese. Season with salt and pepper. Whisk until the cheese melts. Arrange the potatoes and onions in a 9×13-inch baking dish. Top with the cream mixture. Layer the provolone cheese on top and sprinkle with the parsley. Bake, covered, at 350 degrees for 1 1/2 hours.

Serves 10 to 12 servings

THE FRUIT OF SILENCE IS PRAYER.

THE FRUIT OF PRAYER IS FAITH.

THE FRUIT OF FAITH IS LOVE.

THE FRUIT OF LOVE IS SERVICE.

—*Mother Theresa of Calcutta*

Potatoes Lyonnaise

4 potatoes, cut into 1/4-inch slices
1 (10-ounce) can chicken broth
1/3 cup vegetable oil
2 tablespoons white wine vinegar
2 teaspoons grainy mustard
Salt and pepper to taste
Chopped fresh parsley

Combine the potatoes and broth in a saucepan. Bring to a boil. Reduce the heat
and simmer for 10 minutes or just until the potatoes are tender. Drain the potatoes,
reserving 1/4 cup of the broth. Place the potatoes in a bowl. Whisk the reserved
broth, oil, vinegar and grainy mustard in a small bowl and season with salt and
pepper. Pour over the potatoes and toss gently to coat. Sprinkle with parsley. Serve
warm or at room temperature.

Serves 4

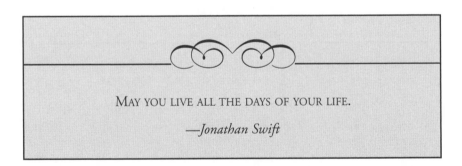

MAY YOU LIVE ALL THE DAYS OF YOUR LIFE.

—*Jonathan Swift*

Grated Potato Casserole

1 cup milk
3 eggs
1 1/2 teaspoons salt
1/8 teaspoon pepper
1 cup cubed Velveeta cheese
2 tablespoons margarine, softened
1/2 bell pepper, cut into pieces
1 small onion, quartered
4 potatoes, peeled and cut into pieces

Combine the milk and eggs in a blender container. Add the salt, pepper, cheese, margarine, bell pepper, onion and potatoes in the order listed. Process at high speed just until the potatoes are finely chopped. Pour into a greased 1 1/2-quart casserole. Bake at 350 degrees for 1 hour.

Serves 6

AFFIRMATION OF LIFE IS THE SPIRITUAL ACT BY WHICH
MAN CEASES TO LIVE UNREFLECTIVELY AND BEGINS TO DEVOTE
HIMSELF TO HIS LIFE WITH REVERENCE IN ORDER TO RAISE
IT TO ITS TRUE VALUE. TO AFFIRM LIFE IS TO DEEPEN. TO MAKE
MORE INWARD, AND TO EXALT THE WILL TO LIVE.

—*Albert Schweitzer*

Four-Cheese Mashed Potatoes with Wild Mushrooms

3 tablespoons butter
2 cups chopped wild mushrooms
    (such as chanterelle, cremini, morel,
    oyster or shiitake)
1/2 cup chopped green onions
6 or 7 russet potatoes, peeled and
    cut into 1/2-inch cubes
1/2 cup soft garlic and herb cheese
1/2 cup shredded provolone cheese
1/2 cup shredded fontina cheese
1/2 cup grated Parmesan cheese
1/2 cup warm milk

Melt the butter in a 10-inch skillet. Add the mushrooms and green onions and sauté for 3 to 4 minutes or until the vegetables are tender. Remove from the heat and keep warm. Cook the potatoes in a large saucepan of boiling water for 18 minutes or until tender. Drain in a colander and return to the saucepan. Mash with a potato masher. Add the garlic and herb cheese, provolone cheese, fontina cheese and Parmesan cheese. Stir until the cheese melts. Add the milk and stir until creamy. Stir in the mushroom mixture. Remove to a serving bowl and top with additional grated cheese, if desired. Serve immediately.

Serves 6 to 8

Spinach Sophia

1/2 cup (1 stick) butter
1 onion, chopped
4 (10-ounce) packages frozen chopped spinach,
    thawed, drained and squeezed dry
1 cup half-and-half
3 hard-cooked eggs, chopped (optional)
2 (10-ounce) cans condensed
    cream of mushroom soup
8 ounces sharp Cheddar cheese, shredded
Paprika

Melt the butter in a skillet. Add the onion and sauté until tender. Remove to a baking dish. Add the spinach and half-and-half. Stir to mix well and spread evenly in the baking dish. Top with the chopped eggs. Spread the soup over the eggs. Top with the cheese and sprinkle with paprika. Bake at 375 degrees for 40 minutes. Stir before serving.

Serves 6 to 8

NOTE: This recipe can be made 1 day ahead. Cover and chill. Reheat before serving. You may add cooked chicken or cooked shrimp when adding the eggs to make a delicious main dish.

spinach stroganoff

2 tablespoons butter
1 bunch green onions, chopped
2 (10-ounce) packages frozen chopped spinach,
  cooked and well drained
1 (10-ounce) can condensed
  cream of mushroom soup
1 cup sour cream
1 (4-ounce) can sliced mushrooms, drained
2 tablespoons chopped fresh parsley
1 tablespoon lemon juice
1 teaspoon Worcestershire sauce
1/4 teaspoon garlic powder
Salt and pepper to taste

Melt the butter in a skillet. Add the green onions and sauté until tender. Remove to a large bowl. Add the spinach, soup, sour cream, mushrooms, parsley, lemon juice, Worcestershire sauce and garlic powder. Season with salt and pepper. Stir to mix well. Pour into a 2-quart baking dish coated with nonstick cooking spray. Bake at 350 degrees for 30 minutes.

Serves 4 to 6

COURAGE IS NOT THE LACK OF FEAR. IT IS ACTING IN SPITE OF IT.

—*Mark Twain*

Baked Cushaw

1 cushaw, cut into pieces and seeds removed
2 eggs, beaten
1 1/2 cups sugar
2 tablespoons all-purpose flour
1/2 teaspoon baking powder
3/4 cup (1 1/2 sticks) butter, melted
1 teaspoon vanilla extract
Nutmeg to taste

Cook the cushaw in a saucepan of boiling water until tender. Drain and peel. Combine the cushaw, eggs, sugar, flour and baking powder in a large bowl and stir to mix. Stir in the melted butter and vanilla and season with nutmeg. Pour into a baking dish. Bake at 350 degrees until golden brown.

Serves 4 to 6

THERE IS A LAND OF THE LIVING AND A LAND OF
THE DEAD, AND THE BRIDGE IS LOVE.

—Thornton Wilder

Squash casserole

1 1/2 pounds yellow squash
Salt and pepper to taste
1 small package herb-seasoned stuffing mix
1/2 cup (1 stick) butter, melted
1 (2-ounce) jar diced pimento, drained
1 (10-ounce) can condensed
    cream of chicken soup
1 cup sour cream
2 tablespoons butter
1 onion, finely chopped

Cook the squash in a saucepan of boiling water until tender; drain. Mash in a large
bowl. Season with salt and pepper. Combine the stuffing mix and 1/2 cup melted
butter in a bowl. Stir to mix well. Add 1/2 of the stuffing mixture to the squash.
Add the pimento, soup and sour cream. Stir to mix well. Melt 2 tablespoons butter
in a skillet. Add the onion and sauté until tender. Add to the squash mixture and
stir to mix well. Spread 1/2 of the remaining stuffing mixture in the bottom of a
greased casserole. Top with the squash mixture. Sprinkle with the remaining stuffing
mixture. Bake at 350 degrees for 30 minutes.

Serves 8

NOTE: This recipe can be made 1 day ahead. Cover and chill. Reheat
before serving.

Praline Sweet Potatoes

3 cups mashed cooked sweet potatoes
1/2 cup sugar
1/2 cup (1 stick) butter, softened
2 eggs, beaten
1 1/2 teaspoons vanilla extract
1/2 cup half-and-half
1/2 cup crushed pineapple
Topping (below)

Combine the sweet potatoes, sugar, butter, eggs, vanilla, half-and-half and pineapple in a large bowl. Stir to mix well. Pour into a greased baking dish. Pour the Topping over the sweet potato mixture. Bake at 350 degrees for 30 minutes.

Serves 6

Topping

1/2 cup half-and-half
1 cup packed dark brown sugar
5 1/3 tablespoons butter, melted
1 cup chopped pecans

Heat the half-and-half in a saucepan until warm. Add the brown sugar. Cook over medium-high heat for 8 to 10 minutes or until the brown sugar dissolves, stirring constantly. Add the melted butter and pecans. Cook until the mixture turns cloudy and is heated through, stirring constantly.

Sweet Potato Casserole

3/4 cup (1 1/2 sticks) butter, softened
3/4 cup sugar
2 eggs, beaten
2 (30-ounce) cans yams, well drained
*   and mashed*
1 teaspoon vanilla extract
1 teaspoon ground cinnamon
1 (3-ounce) can flaked coconut
1 (12-ounce) can evaporated milk
Topping (below)

Beat the butter and sugar in a bowl until light and fluffy. Beat in the eggs. Add the yams, vanilla, cinnamon, coconut and evaporated milk. Stir to mix well. The mixture will be thin. Pour into a nonstick 9×13-inch baking pan. Bake at 350 degrees for 20 to 30 minutes. Sprinkle with the Topping. Bake at 375 degrees for 15 minutes or until the topping is golden brown.

Serves 12 to 15

Topping

1 cup crushed cornflakes
1 cup packed brown sugar
1 (3-ounce) can flaked coconut
1 cup chopped pecans
3/4 cup (1 1/2 sticks) butter, melted

Mix the crushed cornflakes, brown sugar, coconut and pecans in a bowl. Add the butter and stir to mix well.

Tomato Pie

1 (1-crust) pie pastry
4 tomatoes, sliced
Lemon pepper to taste
Basil to taste
Oregano to taste
5 green onions, sliced
2 cups (8 ounces) shredded cheese
Mayonnaise

Flour both sides of the pie pastry. Fit into a pie plate and trim the edge. Prick with a fork. Bake at 350 degrees for 15 minutes. Remove to a wire rack. Arrange the tomato slices in the pie shell. Season with lemon pepper, basil and oregano. Sprinkle with the green onions. Mix the cheese with enough mayonnaise in a bowl to a spreadable consistency. Spread over the green onions. Bake at 350 degrees for 20 minutes. Remove to a wire rack.

Serves 6

[MAN] IS IMMORTAL, NOT BECAUSE HE ALONE AMONG
CREATURES HAS AN INEXHAUSTIBLE VOICE, BUT
BECAUSE HE HAS A SOUL, A SPIRIT CAPABLE OF COMPASSION
AND SACRIFICE AND ENDURANCE.

—*William Faulkner*

Tomatoes Rockefeller

5 large tomatoes, halved
1 (10-ounce) package frozen chopped spinach,
    cooked and well drained
2/3 cup seasoned bread crumbs
1/4 cup chopped green onions
1 egg, lightly beaten
2 tablespoons crumbled crisp-cooked bacon
1/4 cup (1 ounce) grated Parmesan cheese
1/2 cup (1 stick) butter, melted
1 teaspoon lemon juice
1/2 teaspoon salt
1/4 teaspoon garlic powder
3 drops hot red pepper sauce

Arrange the tomatoes, cut side up, on a greased 10×15-inch baking pan. Combine the spinach, bread crumbs, green onions, egg, bacon, cheese, butter, lemon juice, salt, garlic powder and hot sauce in a bowl. Stir to mix well. Mound the spinach mixture on top of each tomato half. Bake at 350 degrees for 30 to 45 minutes.

Serves 8 to 10

zucchini casserole

6 zucchini, sliced
1/4 cup (1/2 stick) butter or
  margarine
1 onion, chopped
3 slices Swiss cheese
1/2 cup sour cream
Salt and pepper taste
Grated Parmesan cheese

Cook the zucchini in a saucepan of boiling water for 10 minutes; drain. Melt the butter in a large saucepan. Add the onion and sauté until tender. Add the Swiss cheese. Cook until the cheese melts, stirring often. Add the sour cream and zucchini and season with salt and pepper. Stir to mix well. Pour into a casserole and sprinkle with Parmesan cheese. Bake at 350 degrees for 30 minutes.

Serves 6

THREE THINGS ARE NECESSARY FOR THE SALVATION OF MAN: TO KNOW
WHAT HE OUGHT TO BELIEVE; TO KNOW WHAT HE OUGHT TO
DESIRE; AND TO KNOW WHAT HE OUGHT TO DO.

—*St. Thomas Aquinas*

Zucchini Tomato Bake

1 pound eggplant, coarsely chopped
2 cups sliced zucchini
2 cup sliced mushrooms
2 teaspoons olive oil
$^1/_2$ cup chopped onion
2 garlic cloves, minced
1 (14-ounce) can whole tomatoes,
   no salt added
1 tablespoon tomato paste
2 teaspoons basil
1 teaspoon sugar

Layer the eggplant, zucchini and mushrooms in a 9×9-inch baking dish. Heat the olive oil in a skillet over medium heat. Add the onion and garlic and sauté for 3 to 4 minutes or until the onion is tender. Stir in the tomatoes, tomato paste, basil and sugar. Cook for 4 minutes or until the sauce thickens, stirring constantly. Pour over the eggplant mixture. Bake, covered, at 350 degrees for 30 minutes. Let cool slightly before serving.

Serves 6

Ratatouille

5$^{1}/_{3}$ tablespoons butter
2 pounds zucchini, cut into $^{1}/_{2}$-inch slices
2 pounds eggplant, peeled and
    cut into $^{1}/_{2}$-inch slices
3 bell peppers, thinly sliced
2 onions, sliced
3 garlic cloves
2 pounds tomatoes, peeled, seeded and sliced
Salt and pepper to taste
1 teaspoon basil
1 teaspoon thyme
1 teaspoon ground bay leaves

Melt the butter in a large skillet. Add the zucchini and eggplant, a few slices at a time, and cook for a few minutes on each side. Remove to paper towels to drain. Add the bell peppers, onions and garlic to the skillet. Sauté for 10 minutes. Remove and discard the garlic. Add the tomatoes to the skillet. Sauté for a few minutes. Arrange $^{1}/_{2}$ of the zucchini and $^{1}/_{2}$ of the eggplant in a baking dish. Top with $^{1}/_{2}$ of the tomato mixture. Season with salt and pepper. Sprinkle with $^{1}/_{2}$ of the basil, $^{1}/_{2}$ of the thyme and $^{1}/_{2}$ of the bay leaves. Top with the remaining zucchini and eggplant and the remaining tomato mixture. Season with salt and pepper. Sprinkle with the remaining basil, thyme and bay leaves. Bake, covered, at 350 degrees for 1 hour.

Serves 8 to 12

Fall vegetables

6 red-skinned potatoes, quartered
2 large sweet potatoes, peeled and cubed
2 cups fresh brussels sprouts, halved
1 cup baby carrots
1 cup pearl onions
2 tablespoons olive oil
1/2 teaspoon salt
1/4 teaspoon pepper
1/4 teaspoon crushed rosemary

Combine the red-skinned potatoes, sweet potatoes, brussels sprouts, carrots, onions, olive oil, salt, pepper and rosemary in a large bowl. Toss gently to mix. Spread in a foil-lined baking pan. Bake at 425 degrees for 30 minutes or until the potatoes are tender.

Serves 6

COURAGE, IT WOULD SEEM, IS NOTHING LESS THAN THE
POWER TO OVERCOME DANGER, MISFORTUNE, FEAR, INJUSTICE,
WHILE CONTINUING TO AFFIRM INWARDLY THAT LIFE WITH
ALL ITS SORROWS IS GOOD; THAT EVERYTHING IS MEANINGFUL EVEN
IF IN A SENSE BEYOND OUR UNDERSTANDING; AND THAT
THERE IS ALWAYS A TOMORROW.

—Dorothy Thompson

Fettuccine Alfredo

1/2 cup (1 stick) butter
2/3 cup heavy cream
1 cup (4 ounces) grated Parmesan cheese
Salt and pepper to taste
9 to 16 ounces fettuccini
1/4 cup (1 ounce) grated Parmesan cheese

Heat the butter and cream in a saucepan until the butter melts, stirring occasionally. Remove from the heat and stir in 1 cup Parmesan cheese. Stir until the cheese melts and the sauce is smooth. Season with salt and pepper. Cook the pasta according to the package directions; drain. Remove the pasta to a large bowl. Add the sauce and toss to coat. Sprinkle with 1/4 cup Parmesan cheese and serve immediately.

Serves 4 to 6

IF WE HAD NO WINTER, THE SPRING WOULD NOT

BE SO PLEASANT; IF WE DID NOT SOMETIMES TASTE OF ADVERSITY,

PROSPERITY WOULD NOT BE SO WELCOME.

—Anne Bradstreet

Home-Style Macaroni and Cheese

1/4 cup (1/2 stick) butter
1 tablespoon all-purpose flour
2 cups milk
8 ounces cream cheese, softened
1 teaspoon Cajun seasoning
2 teaspoons Dijon mustard
7 ounces elbow macaroni, cooked
    al dente and drained
2 cups cubed Velveeta cheese

Melt the butter in a saucepan. Stir in the flour. Cook for a few minutes, stirring
constantly. Stir in the milk gradually. Cook over medium heat until smooth, stirring
occasionally. Stir in the cream cheese, Cajun seasoning and Dijon mustard. Cook
until thickened, stirring constantly. Combine the macaroni and Velveeta cheese in a
large bowl. Add the sauce and stir to mix well. Pour into a greased baking dish.
Bake at 400 degrees for 15 to 20 minutes.

Serves 6

Baked Cheese Grits

1 cup grits
4 cups boiling water
1 teaspoon salt
¹/2 cup (1 stick) margarine
1 (6-ounce) roll garlic cheese
2 eggs
Milk
Cornflake crumbs

Cook the grits with the boiling water and salt in a saucepan according to the package directions. Add the margarine and cheese. Cook until melted, stirring constantly. Remove from the heat and let cool. Break the eggs into a 1-cup measuring cup and beat. Add enough milk to meaasure 1 cup. Beat into the grits mixture. Pour into a greased baking dish. Cover generously with cornflake crumbs. Bake at 350 degrees for 45 minutes to 1 hour. This recipe can be prepared ahead of time and refrigerated until baking time. Increase the baking time accordingly. Leftovers can be reheated by adding a little light cream or milk and returning to the oven.

Serves 8

WISE MEN PROFIT MORE FROM FOOLS THAN FOOLS FROM WISE MEN; FOR THE WISE MEN SHUN THE MISTAKES OF FOOLS, BUT FOOLS DO NOT IMITATE THE SUCCESSES OF THE WISE.

—*Marcus Porcius Cato*

Eggplant Rice Dressing

1 to 2 tablespoons olive oil
2 onions, chopped
1 bell pepper chopped
1 bunch celery, chopped
1/4 cup chopped fresh parsley
1 tablespoon minced garlic
2 pounds ground beef
1 pound hot bulk pork sausage
1 to 2 tablespoons olive oil
2 eggplant, peeled and
   cut into chunks
1 pound mushrooms, sliced

2 1/2 tablespoons Cajun seasoning
   (or to taste)
3 to 4 tablespoons Worcestershire sauce
3 bay leaves
1 (6-ounce) can Dawn Fresh
   Mushroom & Steak Sauce
1 (8-ounce) can water chestnuts,
   drained and coarsely chopped
3 to 4 cups cooked basmati rice
1 bunch green onion tops, chopped

Heat 1 to 2 tablespoons olive oil in a large cast-iron saucepan. Add the onions, bell pepper, celery, parsley and garlic and sauté until the vegetables are tender. Add the ground beef and sausage and cook, stirring until the meat is crumbly and cooked through; drain. Heat 1 to 2 tablespoons olive oil in a skillet. Add the eggplant and sauté until tender. Add to the meat mixture. Stir in the mushrooms, Cajun seasoning, Worcestershire sauce, bay leaves, steak sauce and water chestnuts. Cook for at least 1 hour, stirring occasionally. Discard the bay leaves. Stir in the rice, 1 cup at a time, when ready to serve. Sprinkle with the onion tops.

Serves 8

Patio Rice

1 tablespoon vegetable oil
8 ounces ground beef
1 cup rice
1 (16-ounce) can diced tomatoes
1 teaspoon chili powder
2 teaspoons salt (or to taste)
1¹/₂ teaspoons pepper (or to taste)
2 onions, sliced into rings
2 bell peppers, sliced into rings

Heat the oil in a skillet. Add the ground beef and brown until cooked through and in small chunks; drain. Stir in the rice, tomatoes, chili powder, salt and pepper. Arrange the onions and bell peppers on top. Bring to a boil. Reduce the heat and cover. Cook for 45 minutes. Toss gently before serving.

Serves 4 to 6

I WANTED A PERFECT ENDING. NOW I'VE LEARNED, THE HARD WAY,
THAT SOME POEMS DON'T RHYME, AND SOME STORIES DON'T
HAVE A CLEAR BEGINNING, MIDDLE, AND END. LIFE IS ABOUT NOT
KNOWING, HAVING TO CHANGE, TAKING THE MOMENT AND
MAKING THE BEST OF IT, WITHOUT KNOWING WHAT'S GOING TO
HAPPEN NEXT. DELICIOUS AMBIGUITY.

—*Gilda Radner*

seafood

Fear not
The unknown
For you
My friend
Are never Alone.
L LaBorde

Kim's beloved grandmother had died two years ago. Kim and she had shared a special bond, and Kim had spent many weekends at Granny's house. Granny would often swing Kim in a tire swing in the backyard of her house. Kim—now an adult, married and with a seven-year-old child of her own—was in intensive care and dying as the result of a pulmonary problem. She was on the ventilator, and neither lung was functioning. As she lay in her bed with her mother at her bedside, she "dreamed" of her grandmother pushing her in the tire swing. As she swung back toward her grandmother, she felt joy and peace and begged her grandmother to let her stay. Instead, her grandmother pushed her away and told her, "You have a son to raise, and your time on earth is not finished. You will have another son, and you need to stay to raise both of your boys."

In the morning, Kim's lungs had miraculously both cleared, and she was removed from the ventilator and was on her way to full recovery. The following year, she gave birth to her second son. She knows her grandmother is watching over all of them until they see her again.

—Pat Lejeune, R.N.

ARTIST: LAURA LABORDE—"NEVER ALONE"
Submitted in memory of her dear Dad, Alexander Duffus

Laura's words on the bottom left-hand corner of this painting read: "Fear not the unknown for you my friend are never alone." She comes to Louisiana from Scotland. She teaches art from a home studio to children and adults as well as teaching art at The Greenhouse, a center for Senior Citizens in Lafayette.

Salmon à la Crème au Vin

4 tomatoes, peeled, seeded and diced
2 shallots, chopped
1 1/2 cups dry white wine
1/2 teaspoon salt
1/2 teaspoon white pepper
2/3 cup crème fraiche
3 tablespoons butter
6 center-cut salmon fillets, skinned
1/2 teaspoon salt
1/2 teaspoon white pepper
1 teaspoon finely chopped fresh chervil or parsley
1 teaspoon finely chopped fresh chives
1 teaspoon finely chopped fresh tarragon

Combine the tomatoes, shallots, wine, 1/2 teaspoon salt and 1/2 teaspoon white pepper in a saucepan. Cook over medium heat for 10 minutes or until reduced by 1/3, stirring occasionally. Strain through a fine mesh sieve, pressing to extract all the liquid. Discard the solids. Return the liquid to the saucepan and stir in the crème fraiche. Adjust the seasonings. Cook for 2 to 3 minutes or until slightly thickened, stirring often. Heat the butter in a large skillet over medium-high heat until foamy. Add the salmon and cook for 2 minutes or until golden brown. Turn the salmon and cook for 2 minutes or until golden brown on the other side. Sprinkle with 1/2 teaspoon salt and 1/2 teaspoon white pepper. Pour the sauce over the salmon and sprinkle with the chervil, chives and tarragon. Serve immediately.

Serves 6

NOTE: You may use 1/3 cup sour cream and 1/3 cup heavy cream instead of the crème fraiche.

Trout Meunière

4 trout fillets or other mild fish fillets
Creole seasoning to taste
1 cup all-purpose flour
Salt and pepper to taste
1 (5-ounce) can evaporated milk
$^{1}/_{2}$ cup canola oil
$^{1}/_{4}$ cup ($^{1}/_{2}$ stick) butter
$^{1}/_{4}$ cup chopped pecans (optional)
Juice of 1 lemon
$^{1}/_{4}$ cup dry sherry
2 tablespoons chopped green onions
1 tablespoon chopped fresh parsley

Season the fish with Creole seasoning. Season the flour with salt and pepper. Dip the fish in the evaporated milk and coat in the flour. Let stand for 10 minutes. Heat the canola oil and butter in a large skillet over medium-high heat. Add the fish and cook for 5 minutes or until golden brown. Turn the fish and cook the other side until golden brown and the fish flakes easily. Remove to a serving platter and keep warm. Add the pecans to the skillet. Stir in the lemon juice and sherry. Stir in additional flour if needed to make a thickened sauce. Cook for 2 to 3 minutes, stirring constantly. Pour the sauce over the fish. Sprinkle with the green onions and parsley.

Serves 4

Pecan-Encrusted Speckled Trout

3 tablespoons butter
6 tablespoons chopped green onions
2 teaspoons all-purpose flour
1 cup dry white wine
1 cup half-and-half
1 teaspoon salt
1/4 teaspoon Tabasco sauce
1/4 teaspoon garlic salt
1/4 cup (1/2 stick) butter
1 cup finely chopped pecans
1/2 cup bread crumbs
4 large or 6 small speckled trout fillets
Paprika

Melt 3 tablespoons butter in a saucepan. Add the green onions and sauté until tender. Stir in the flour. Cook for 1 minute, stirring constantly. Reduce the heat to low and stir in the wine, half-and-half, salt, Tabasco sauce and garlic salt. Cook until slightly thickened, stirring often. Melt 1/4 cup butter in a skillet. Add the pecans and sauté until toasted. Stir in the bread crumbs. Arrange the fish in a greased baking dish. Pour the sauce over the fish. Top with the pecan mixture and sprinkle with paprika. Bake at 375 degrees for 10 to 15 minutes or until the fish flakes easily.

Serves 4 to 6

Light Trout Amandine Dinner

1 cup sliced almonds
8 speckled trout fillets
Butter-flavor nonstick cooking spray
Cajun seasoning to taste
1 cup all-purpose flour
1 lemon, quartered

Spread the almonds on a microwave-safe plate. Microwave for 1 minute or until toasted, stirring occasionally. Rinse the fish and pat dry. Coat both sides of the fish with cooking spray. Season with Cajun seasoning and coat in the flour. Coat the fish with cooking spray again. Coat a hot skillet with cooking spray. Add the fish and cook for 4 minutes or until golden brown. Turn the fish and sprinkle with the almonds. Cook the other side until golden brown and the fish flakes easily. Serve immediately with the lemon.

Serves 4

NOTE: You may use any thin fish fillet, such as flounder, catfish or tilapia, in this recipe.

FLATTER ME, AND I MAY NOT BELIEVE YOU. CRITICIZE ME,
AND I MAY NOT LIKE YOU. IGNORE ME, AND I MAY NOT FORGIVE YOU.
ENCOURAGE ME, AND I WILL NOT FORGET YOU.

—William Arthur Ward

Trout Fillets with Crab Meat Sauce

1/4 cup (1/2 stick) butter
1/2 cup finely chopped shallots or
   green onions
3 tablespoons all-purpose flour
1/2 cup milk
1 cup sour cream
1 pound lump crab meat
6 (6-ounce) trout fillets
Melted butter
Salt and pepper to taste
Chopped fresh parsley
Lemon wedges
Paprika

Melt 1/4 cup butter in a saucepan. Add the shallots and sauté until tender. Stir in the flour. Cook for a few minutes, stirring constantly. Do not brown. Stir in the milk. Cook until thickened, stirring constantly. Stir in the sour cream and crab meat. Remove from the heat. Arrange the fish on a greased baking sheet or in a greased baking dish. Brush with melted butter. Season with salt and pepper. Spoon an equal amount of the crab meat sauce on each fillet. Bake at 350 degrees for 30 minutes or until the fish flakes easily. Serve garnished with parsley, lemon and paprika.

Serve 6.

Redfish Moreau

2 (8-ounce) redfish fillets
Salt to taste
White pepper to taste
Cayenne pepper to taste
Garlic to taste
2 eggs
1 cup half-and-half
1/2 cup (1 stick) unsalted butter
1 cup all-purpose flour
1 cup heavy cream
1/4 cup chopped green onions
1/2 cup sliced mushrooms
1/2 teaspoon cayenne pepper
1/4 teaspoon salt
1/4 teaspoon white pepper
1/4 teaspoon minced garlic
1 teaspoon paprika
6 ounces crawfish, cooked, peeled and seasoned to taste

Season the fish generously with salt, white pepper, cayenne pepper and garlic.
Beat the eggs and half-and-half in a shallow bowl. Season with salt, white pepper,
cayenne pepper and garlic. Melt the butter in a skillet over medium heat. Dip the
fish into the egg mixture and coat in the flour. Add to the melted butter and cook
for 3 minutes per side or until the fish flakes easily. Remove to serving plates and
keep warm. Combine the cream, green onions, mushrooms, 1/2 teaspoon cayenne
pepper, 1/4 teaspoon salt, 1/4 teaspoon white pepper and 1/4 teaspoon minced garlic
in a skillet. Cook over high heat for 3 minutes or until thickened, stirring
constantly. Stir in the paprika and remove from the heat. Stir in the crawfish. Pour
over the fish.

Serves 2

Redfish Court-Bouillon

1/2 cup vegetable oil or melted butter
1/2 cup all-purpose flour
1/2 cup chopped onion
1 cup chopped celery
1 cup chopped bell pepper
1 tablespoon minced garlic
1 cup water
1 cup chicken broth
2 cups tomato sauce
4 cups canned stewed tomatoes
Salt, black pepper and cayenne pepper to taste
1 1/2 to 2 pounds redfish fillets,
   cut into 2- to 3-inch cubes
1/4 cup chopped green onions
2 tablespoons chopped fresh parsley
Hot cooked rice

Mix the oil and flour in a large heavy saucepan or Dutch oven. Cook over medium heat for 30 to 45 minutes or until dark chocolate colored brown, stirring constantly. Add the onion, celery, bell pepper and garlic and sauté until the vegetables are tender, stirring constantly. Stir in the water, chicken broth, tomato sauce and tomatoes. Bring to a boil, stirring constantly. Season with salt, black pepper and cayenne pepper. Reduce the heat to medium-low and simmer for 45 minutes, stirring occasionally. Stir in the fish, green onions and parsley. Cook for 15 minutes. Reduce the heat to low. Cook for 15 minutes longer or until the fish flakes easily. Serve over rice.

Serves 6 to 8

NOTE: You may use any firm white fish in this recipe.

Bouillabaisse

Vegetable oil
4 to 5 pounds redfish, red snapper
*   or grouper fillets*
1 or 2 onions, chopped
2 ribs celery, chopped
1 bell pepper, chopped
2 garlic cloves, chopped
1 can crushed tomatoes
Cajun seasoning to taste or salt
*   and pepper to taste*
Hot cooked rice

Cover the bottom of a large cast-iron saucepan with oil. Starting with the larger pieces of fish, add layers of fish, onions, celery, bell pepper, garlic and tomatoes, seasoning each layer with Cajun seasoning. Cook, covered, over low heat for 45 to 60 minutes or until the fish is opaque. Do not stir, but gently shake the pot every 10 to 15 minutes. Serve over rice.

Serves 8 to 10

VIRTUE IS NOT LEFT TO STAND ALONE. HE WHO

PRACTICES IT WILL HAVE NEIGHBORS.

—Confucius

Pecan-Topped Snapper

2 small red snapper
Salt and a variety of peppers to taste
1 tablespoon oregano
1 tablespoon tarragon
3 to 4 tablespoons olive oil
Dry white wine
2 to 3 tablespoons butter
2 to 3 tablespoons olive oil
6 to 8 tablespoons chopped pecans

Wash the fish and pat dry. Season with salt and peppers. Mix the oregano, tarragon and 3 to 4 tablespoons olive oil in a small bowl. Spread on both sides of the fish. Drizzle with a small amount of wine. Chill, covered, for at least 1 hour. Heat the butter and 2 to 3 tablespoons olive oil in a nonstick skillet over medium-low heat. Add the pecans and sauté until toasted. Push the pecans to one side of the skillet. Add the fish and increase the heat to medium-high. Cook until golden brown. Turn the fish and add a small amount of wine to the skillet, if desired. Cook the other side until golden brown and the fish flakes easily. Top with the pecans and serve immediately.

Serves 2 to 4

NOTE: You may use trout fillets, red snapper fillets or skinned flounder instead of whole red snapper.

voodoo Fish with Jamaican Salsa

3 tablespoons chopped fresh cilantro
1 jalapeño chile, seeded and chopped
2 tablespoons fresh lime juice
1 tablespoon minced garlic
1 tablespoon finely chopped fresh ginger
4 (8-ounce) red snapper fillets
Jamaican Salsa (below)

Mix the cilantro, jalapeño, lime juice, garlic and ginger in a small bowl. Coat a grill rack with nonstick cooking spray. Heat over hot coals or a 400- to 500-degree grill for 10 minutes, with the grill lid closed. Place the fish on the grill. Cook for 10 minutes with the grill lid closed. Turn the fish and spread each fillet with the cilantro mixture. Cook with the grill lid closed for 10 minutes or until the fish flakes easily. Serve with Jamaican Salsa.

Serves 4

Jamaican Salsa

1 large banana, chopped
1/2 cup finely chopped red bell pepper
1/2 cup finely chopped green bell pepper
1/2 cup chopped fresh cilantro
3 green onions, finely chopped
1 jalapeño chile, seeded and chopped
3 tablespoons fresh lime juice
2 tablespoons brown sugar
1 tablespoon finely chopped fresh ginger
1 tablespoon olive oil
1/4 teaspoon each salt and pepper

Combine the banana, red bell pepper, green bell pepper, cilantro, green onions, jalapeño, lime juice, brown sugar, ginger, olive oil, salt and pepper in a bowl. Stir to mix well.

Island Snapper

1 (6- to 8-ounce) red snapper fillet
Seasonings to taste
All-purpose flour for dredging
Cajun seasoning to taste
1 egg
1/2 cup milk
5 tablespoons unsalted butter
3 tablespoons lime juice
1/2 cup diced banana
1/2 cup diced pineapple
1/4 cup toasted pecans, chopped

Season the fish as desired. Season the flour with Cajun seasoning. Beat the egg and milk in a shallow dish. Dredge the fish in the flour. Dip in the egg mixture and dredge in the flour again. Melt 2 tablespoons of the butter in a skillet. Add the fish and cook for a few minutes. Turn the fish and cook the other side until the fish flakes easily. Remove to a serving platter and keep warm. Melt the remaining 3 tablespoons butter in a skillet. Add the lime juice, banana, pineapple and pecans. Cook until the fruit is heated through and the juice is thickened, stirring constantly. Pour over the fish and serve.

Serves 3 to 4

NOT EVERYTHING THAT IS FACED CAN BE CHANGED, BUT NOTHING
CAN BE CHANGED UNTIL IT IS FACED.

—*James Baldwin*

Crab Meat Au Gratin

1/4 cup (1/2 stick) margarine
2 tablespoons all-purpose flour
1 cup milk
1 tablespoon margarine
1/2 onion, finely chopped
2 ribs celery, chopped
3 tablespoons chopped bell pepper
1 garlic clove, minced
1 pound crab meat, drained and flaked
1 cup cubed jalapeño Velveeta cheese
1 cup bread crumbs
Seasonings to taste

Melt 1/4 cup margarine in a saucepan. Stir in the flour. Cook for a few minutes, stirring constantly. Stir in the milk. Cook until thickened, stirring constantly. Remove from the heat. Melt 1 tablespoon margarine in a saucepan. Add the onion, celery, bell pepper and garlic and sauté until the vegetables are tender. Add the crab meat, cheese and 1/2 of the bread crumbs. Season to taste. Stir to mix well. Pour into a baking dish. Top with the remaining bread crumbs. Bake at 350 degrees for 30 minutes.

Serves 4

ONE WORD FREES US OF ALL THE WEIGHT AND

PAIN OF LIFE: THAT WORD IS LOVE.

—*Sophocles*

Crab Dressing

1/2 loaf French bread, thinly sliced
2 cups (about) water or seafood stock
1 cup (2 sticks) butter
3 large onions, coarsely chopped
2 bell peppers, coarsely chopped
2 ribs celery, coarsely chopped
1/2 cup crab fat (optional)
Juice of 3 lemons or 1/4 cup lemon juice
1/4 cup Worcestershire sauce
1 tablespoon salt
1 teaspoon white pepper
2 teaspoons black pepper
2 teaspoons cayenne pepper
2 pounds crab meat, drained and flaked
1 cup chopped green onions
1 cup chopped fresh parsley
Butter and lemon juice

Arrange the bread slices in a single layer on a baking sheet. Bake at 200 degrees for up to 30 minutes to dry; do not brown. Remove to a large bowl and work in enough of the water to make a very thick mash. Melt 1 cup butter in a large saucepan over medium-high heat. Add the onions, bell peppers, celery, crab fat, lemon juice, Worcestershire sauce, salt, white pepper, black pepper and cayenne pepper. Cook for 45 minutes or until the vegetables are very soft, stirring occasionally. Stir in the crab meat and cook for 5 minutes. Reduce the heat to low and stir in the bread mixture. Cook until well mixed, stirring constantly. Remove from the heat. Stir in the green onions and parsley and let cool. Cover and chill for at least 2 hours or up to 4 days. Spoon into ramekins. Dot with butter and sprinkle with lemon juice. Bake at 325 degrees until heated through.

Serves 16

NOTE: Use this dressing in stuffed peppers, stuffed mushrooms, or with seafood. Do not reduce the recipe, but extra dressing freezes well.

crab stew

1 cup vegetable oil	Salt, black pepper and cayenne pepper
1 cup all-purpose flour	to taste
1 onion chopped	Cleaned whole crab bodies and claws
1/2 bell pepper, chopped	Fresh crab meat (optional)
2 garlic cloves, minced	Shrimp (optional)
2 quarts water	Hot cooked rice

Heat the oil in a large heavy saucepan. Stir in the flour. Cook until dark brown, stirring constantly. Stir in the onion, bell pepper and garlic. Stir in the water. Season with salt, black pepper and cayenne pepper. Simmer over low heat for 1 to 1 1/2 hours, stirring occasionally. Clean the crabs by discarding the outer shell and lungs and add to the roux. Add the crab meat and shrimp. Cook for 20 minutes or until the crab is cooked through. Adjust the seasonings. Serve over rice.

Serves 4 to 6

crawfish stew

1 cup (2 sticks) butter	Cayenne pepper to taste
3/4 cup all-purpose flour	2 pounds peeled Louisiana
2 onions, chopped	crawfish tails
2 bell peppers, chopped	2 teaspoons Worcestershire sauce
4 ribs celery, chopped	Hot cooked rice
2 garlic cloves, minced	1/2 cup chopped green onions
Cajun seasoning to taste	

Melt the butter in a large heavy saucepan. Stir in the flour. Cook until medium brown, stirring constantly. Stir in the onions, bell peppers, celery and garlic. Season with Cajun seasoning and cayenne pepper. Simmer for 30 minutes to 1 hour, stirring occasionally. Season the crawfish with Cajun seasoning. Add the crawfish to the saucepan and stir in the Worcestershire sauce. Add enough water to cover the ingredients. Simmer for 1 to 1 1/2 hours, adding more water if needed. Taste and adjust the seasonings. Serve over rice and top with the green onions.

Serves 4 to 6

Crawfish Pies

1 cup chopped onion
1 cup chopped celery
1 bunch green onions, chopped
2 garlic cloves, minced
1/2 cup (1 stick) butter, melted
1 (10-ounce) can each condensed
    cream of onion soup and
    condensed cream of celery soup

1 cup heavy cream
2 pounds crawfish tails
2 tablespoons chopped fresh parsley
Salt and pepper to taste
Pinch of lemon pepper
2 pinches of cayenne pepper
Juice of 1/2 lemon
2 unbaked deep-dish pie shells

Sauté the onion, celery, green onions and garlic in the butter in a large saucepan until tender. Stir in the soups and cream. Cook for 10 minutes. Stir in the crawfish and parsley. Cook for 10 minutes or until the crawfish are tender. Season with salt and pepper. Stir in the lemon pepper, cayenne pepper and lemon juice. Pour into the pie shells. Bake at 350 degrees for 25 to 30 minutes or until golden brown.

Serves 10

Crawfish Étouffée

3/4 cup (1 1/2 sticks) butter
1 onion, chopped
1/2 bell pepper, chopped
3 garlic cloves, minced
1 tablespoon all-purpose flour
1 cup chicken bouillon
1 pound crawfish tails

1 cup dry sherry
1/2 teaspoon butter flavoring
Creole seasoning to taste
1 bunch green onion tops, chopped
1/2 cup chopped fresh parsley
Hot cooked rice

Melt the butter in a large saucepan. Add the onion, bell pepper and garlic and sauté over very low heat for 20 minutes. Stir in the flour. Cook for a few minutes, stirring constantly. Stir in the bouillon. Bring to a boil, stirring constantly. Reduce the heat and stir in the crawfish, sherry and butter flavor. Season with Creole seasoning. Simmer for 25 minutes. Stir in the green onion tops and parsley. Cook for 5 minutes. Serve over rice.

Serves 4

Leslie's Crawfish Fettuccini

1¹/2 cups (3 sticks) margarine
3 onions, finely chopped
2 bell peppers, finely chopped
¹/4 cup all-purpose flour
¹/4 cup dried parsley flakes
3 pounds crawfish tails, peeled
2 cups half-and-half
1 pound jalapeño Velveeta cheese,
   cut into small pieces

2 garlic cloves, minced
10 dashes of Worcestershire sauce
Juice of 1 slice of lemon
Salt, black pepper and cayenne pepper
   to taste
12 ounces fine or medium fettuccini,
   cooked al dente and drained
Grated Parmesan cheese

Melt the margarine in a large saucepan. Stir in the onions and bell peppers. Cook, covered, for 15 to 20 minutes or until the vegetables are tender. Stir in the flour. Cook, covered, for 15 minutes, stirring frequently to prevent sticking. Stir in the parsley and crawfish. Cook, covered, for 15 minutes, stirring frequently to prevent sticking. Stir in the half-and-half, Velveeta cheese, garlic, Worcestershire sauce and lemon juice. Season with salt, black pepper and cayenne pepper. Cook, covered, over low heat for 30 minutes, stirring occasionally. Remove from the heat and add the pasta. Stir to mix well. Pour into 2 greased 3-quart baking dishes or 1 large baking dish. Sprinkle with Parmesan cheese. Bake at 350 degrees for 15 to 20 minutes or until heated through.

Serves 12

NOTE: Leslie was the Director of Clinical Services for Hospice of Acadiana until her untimely death in November of 2004. She had been with Hospice of Acadiana for eighteen years.

crawfish casserole

1/2 cup (1 stick) butter
1 cup chopped onion
1 cup chopped green bell pepper
1 cup chopped celery
2 garlic cloves, chopped
1 (10-ounce) can condensed
 cream of mushroom soup
1 (10-ounce) can condensed
 Cheddar cheese soup
1/3 cup chopped parsley
1 cup chopped green onions
1 jar diced pimentos, undrained
2 tablespoons hot red pepper sauce
1 teaspoon salt
1 teaspoon pepper
3 cups cooked crawfish, cooked shrimp or
 cooked ground beef
2 cups cooked rice

Melt the butter in a large saucepan. Add the onion, bell pepper, celery and garlic and sauté until the vegetables are tender. Stir in the mushroom soup, cheese soup, parsley, green onions, pimentos, hot sauce, salt and pepper. Stir in the crawfish. Cook until heated through. Stir in the rice. Pour into a 3-quart casserole. Bake at 350 degrees for 30 minutes.

Serves 4 to 6

Shrimp and Andouille Brochettes

1/4 cup dry white vermouth
1 teaspoon white wine vinegar
1 teaspoon chopped shallots
1/2 cup heavy cream or chicken broth
1 tablespoon diced peeled roasted red bell pepper
Tarragon to taste
1 tablespoon butter
1 1/2 teaspoons Creole mustard
1/2 teaspoon Dijon mustard
Salt and cayenne pepper to taste
16 fresh jumbo shrimp
1 large red bell pepper, cut into 1-inch pieces
1 pound andouille, cut into 1/2-inch pieces
Creole seasoning to taste
1/4 cup (1/2 stick) butter, melted
Hot cooked rice

Mix the vermouth, vinegar and shallots in a small heavy saucepan. Boil until reduced to 2 tablespoons. Stir in the cream and 1 tablespoon roasted red bell pepper. Season with tarragon. Boil until reduced to about 1/3 cup. Reduce the heat to medium-low. Whisk in the butter, Creole mustard and Dijon mustard. Cook for 30 seconds, whisking constantly. Season with salt and cayenne pepper and keep warm. Peel and devein the shrimp, leaving the tails attached. Thread the shrimp, bell pepper and andouille alternately onto metal skewers or wooden skewers that have been soaked in water. Sprinkle with Creole seasoning and brush with the melted butter. Grill for 7 minutes or until the shrimp turn pink, turning occasionally and brushing with the melted butter. Spoon the sauce over rice on serving plates. Slide the brochettes off the skewers onto the sauce.

Serves 4

Skewered Shrimp and Andouille

1¹/2 cups (3 sticks) butter
2 tablespoons minced garlic
3 tablespoons Creole mustard or
    other grainy mustard
2 teaspoons Worcestershire sauce
1 teaspoon Tabasco sauce
¹/3 cup lemon juice
Cajun seasoning to taste
1 pound fresh large shrimp
1 pound andouille, cut into ¹/2-inch pieces
1 red onion, cut into 1-inch pieces
1 red bell pepper, cut into 1-inch pieces
1 green bell pepper, cut into 1-inch pieces

Melt the butter in a saucepan. Stir in the garlic, Creole mustard, Worcestershire sauce, Tabasco sauce and lemon juice. Season with Cajun seasoning. Cook until heated through, stirring often. Peel and devein the shrimp, leaving the tails attached. Thread the shrimp, andouille, onion, red bell pepper and green bell pepper alternately onto fifteen 6-inch bamboo skewers that have been soaked in water. Grill or broil until the shrimp turn pink, turning occasionally and basting often with the butter sauce.

Serves 4 to 6

HE IS THE GOD NOT OF THE DEAD BUT OF THE LIVING,

BECAUSE TO HIM ALL ARE ALIVE.

—*Luke 20:38*

Shrimp and Artichoke on Angel Hair Pasta

3/4 cup (1 1/2 sticks) butter
1 tablespoon olive oil
1 bunch green onions, chopped
1 cup vermouth
1 (14-ounce) can artichoke
  hearts, drained
Juice of 1 lemon
1 teaspoon oregano
Salt and pepper to taste
2 to 3 pounds fresh deveined
  peeled shrimp
1 cup sour cream
8 ounces angel hair pasta, cooked
  al dente and drained

Heat the butter and olive oil in a large skillet. Add the green onions and sauté until tender. Stir in the vermouth, artichokes, lemon juice and oregano. Season with salt and pepper. Add the shrimp and sauté until the shrimp turn pink. Stir in the sour cream. Serve over the pasta.

Serves 4

NOTE: You can thicken the sauce with a small amount of a cornstarch and water mixture, if desired.

shrimp and crab sauté

1/2 to 3/4 cup extra-virgin olive oil
2 onions, chopped
2 tablespoons minced fresh garlic
1 cup chopped celery
5 pounds fresh deveined peeled medium shrimp
1 1/2 tablespoons Creole seasoning
1 1/2 tablespoons lemon and herb seasoning
1 1/2 tablespoons basil
1 1/2 tablespoons garlic and herb seasoning
1 1/2 tablespoons Italian seasoning
8 ounces cooked lump crab meat
8 ounces cooked claw crab meat
1 tablespoon hot red pepper sauce
8 ounces sliced mushrooms
1/4 cup (1/2 stick) butter
1/2 cup water
1/2 cup chopped fresh parsley
1/2 cup chopped shallots
Hot cooked angel hair pasta

Heat the olive oil in a large skillet over medium-high heat. Add the onions, garlic and celery and sauté for 10 minutes or until the vegetables are tender. Add the shrimp and sauté for 15 minutes. Stir in the Creole seasoning, lemon and herb seasoning, basil, garlic and herb seasoning and Italian seasoning. Reduce the heat to medium and cook for 15 minutes, stirring occasionally. Stir in the lump crab meat, claw crab meat, hot sauce, mushrooms and butter. Cook for 15 to 20 minutes, stirring occasionally. Add the water and stir to mix well. Stir in the parsley and shallots. Cook for 10 to 15 minutes, stirring occasionally. Serve over pasta.

Serves 6 to 8

shrimp spaghetti

3 tablespoons butter
3 tablespoons olive oil
1 onion, chopped
1 rib celery, chopped
2 or 3 garlic cloves, minced
1 bell pepper, chopped
Chopped green onions
Chopped fresh parsley
1 pound fresh small to medium shrimp
2 teaspoons chicken bouillon granules
2 tablespoons white wine
12 ounces spaghetti, cooked al dente and drained
Salt, black pepper and cayenne pepper to taste

Melt the butter in a large heavy saucepan. Add the olive oil, onion, celery, garlic, bell pepper, green onions and parsley. Sauté until the vegetables are tender. Stir in the shrimp, bouillon granules and wine. Sauté until the shrimp turn pink. Stir in the pasta. Season with salt, black pepper and cayenne pepper.

Serves 4

MAKE FRIENDS WITH THE ANGELS, WHO THOUGH INVISIBLE
ARE ALWAYS WITH YOU. . .OFTEN INVOKE THEM, CONSTANTLY
PRAISE THEM, AND MAKE GOOD USE OF THEIR HELP AND
ASSISTANCE IN ALL YOUR TEMPORAL AND SPIRITUAL AFFAIRS.

—*St. Francis De Sales*

shrimp and pasta

1 1/2 pounds fresh deveined peeled
  shrimp
Seasonings to taste
8 garlic cloves, minced
1/4 cup (1/2 stick) butter
1/4 cup olive oil
2 cups chopped tomatoes

1/2 cup white wine
1/2 teaspoon rosemary
1/2 teaspoon thyme
1/2 teaspoon tarragon
1/2 teaspoon basil
Hot cooked pasta

Season the shrimp generously with desired seasonings. Mix the shrimp and garlic in a bowl. Cover and chill to blend flavors. Melt the butter in a large skillet over low heat. Stir in the olive oil and tomatoes. Cook for 15 minutes. Stir in the wine. Add the shrimp and garlic and cook over medium-low heat for 8 to 10 minutes or until the shrimp turn pink. Stir in the rosemary, thyme, tarragon and basil. Serve over pasta.

Serves 4

DEATH IS NOTHING BUT GOING HOME TO GOD.

—Mother Theresa of Calcutta

Shrimp and Bow Tie Pasta

1 pound fresh shrimp
Seasonings to taste
Olive oil
1 cup prepared pesto
1 package bow tie pasta, cooked al dente and drained
1 head romaine, chopped
1/2 block feta cheese, crumbled
1 red onion, chopped
1 cup creamy Caesar salad dressing
Girard's Champagne salad dressing or bottled Italian salad dressing to taste

Season the shrimp with desired seasonings. Sauté the shrimp in olive oil in a skillet until the shrimp turn pink. Remove to a large bowl. Add the pesto and pasta and toss to mix. Combine the lettuce, cheese, onion and Caesar salad dressing in a large bowl. Add Champagne salad dressing to taste. Toss to mix. Add the pasta mixture. Toss to mix.

Serve 4 to 6

THERE ARE THREE WAYS ONE CAN DIE: "NO!"
"I GUESS I HAVE NO CHOICE!" AND "YES." ONLY THE THIRD
IS A TRULY CHRISTIAN DEATH.

—paraphrase of Karl Rahner

Shrimp Rosmarino

¹/₄ cup extra-virgin olive oil
2 garlic cloves, chopped
2 sprigs rosemary, stems removed
  and leaves chopped
2 pounds fresh shrimp
Salt and pepper to taste

Heat the olive oil in a heavy skillet over medium-high heat. Add the garlic and rosemary and sauté until the garlic is golden brown. Add the shrimp and season with salt and pepper. Sauté just until the shrimp turn pink. Serve immediately with crusty bread.

Serves 4 to 6

I AM NOT DYING. I AM ENTERING INTO LIFE!

—St. Therese of Lisieux

white Beans and Shrimp

1 pound dried white beans
8 ounces bacon, cut into 1/4-inch strips
1 teaspoon liquid crab boil
1 large onion, chopped
2 ribs celery, chopped
2 or 3 green onions, chopped
1/2 bell pepper, chopped
1 garlic clove, minced
1 bay leaf
Salt and pepper to taste
1 pound fresh deveined peeled small shrimp
Hot cooked rice

Cook the beans in a large saucepan of simmering water until tender; drain. Fry
the bacon in a skillet until cooked through but not crisp; drain. Mix the beans
and bacon in a large saucepan. Stir in the crab boil, onion and celery. Cook for
45 minutes, stirring occasionally. Stir in the green onions, bell pepper, garlic and
bay leaf. Season with salt and pepper. Cook until creamy, stirring occasionally. Stir
in the shrimp and cook over low heat for 20 minutes or until the shrimp turn pink.
Discard the bay leaf and serve over rice.

Serves 6

shrimp Jambalaya

1/4 cup vegetable oil
2 large onions, finely chopped
3/4 cup finely chopped celery
3/4 cup finely chopped bell pepper
1/2 cup chopped green onion tops
1/2 cup chopped fresh parsley
2 to 3 teaspoons Creole seasoning
3 to 4 cups fresh shrimp
6 cups water
1 1/2 cups rice

Heat the oil in a large cast-iron saucepan or heavy aluminum saucepan over medium-low heat. Add the onions and sauté until golden brown. Add the celery, bell pepper, green onions, parsley and Creole seasoning and sauté until the vegetables are tender. Stir in shrimp. Cook, covered, until the shrimp turn pink, stirring occasionally. Stir in the water and bring to a boil. Stir in the rice and reduce the heat. Cook until the rice is tender and the water is absorbed.

Serves 4

TOO OFTEN WE UNDERESTIMATE THE POWER OF A TOUCH,
A SMILE, A KIND WORD, A LISTENING EAR, AN HONEST COMPLIMENT,
OR THE SMALLEST ACT OF CARING, ALL OF WHICH HAVE THE
POTENTIAL TO TURN A LIFE AROUND.

—*Leo Buscaglia*

shrimp creole

3 pounds fresh medium heads-on shrimp
4 cups water
1/4 cup vegetable oil
3 onions, chopped
1 bell pepper, chopped
4 ribs celery, chopped
6 tomatoes, peeled, seeded and crushed
2 teaspoons Cajun seasoning
2 teaspoons thyme
2 teaspoons basil
1 teaspoon sugar
4 bay leaves
1 cup chopped green onion tops
1 cup chopped fresh parsley
Hot cooked rice

Peel and devein the shrimp, reserving the heads and peels. Place the heads and peels in a saucepan. Cover and chill the shrimp. Add the water to the shrimp heads and peels. Bring to a boil and reduce the heat to medium. Cook for 20 to 30 minutes. Strain the stock, discarding the solids. Heat the oil in a large saucepan. Add the onions, bell pepper and celery and cook over low heat for 40 minutes, stirring often. Stir in the shrimp stock, tomatoes, Cajun seasoning, thyme, basil, sugar and bay leaves. Cook for 45 minutes, stirring occasionally. Add the shrimp and cook over low heat for 7 to 10 minutes. Stir in the green onions and parsley and cook for 3 to 5 minutes. Discard the bay leaves and serve over rice.

Serves 6 to 8

creole shrimp casserole

3 cups cooked long grain and wild rice mix
2 pounds fresh deveined peeled medium shrimp
1 cup (4 ounces) shredded mild Cheddar cheese
1 (10-ounce) can condensed
 cream of mushroom soup
1 tablespoon butter
1/2 cup chopped green onions
2 teaspoons Worcestershire sauce
1/2 teaspoon dry mustard
1/2 teaspoon freshly ground pepper
1/4 cup milk
Tabasco sauce to taste
Cajun seasoning to taste

Stir the rice, shrimp, cheese and soup in a large bowl. Melt the butter in a skillet.
Add the green onions and sauté until tender. Add to the rice mixture. Add the
Worcestershire sauce, dry mustard, pepper and milk. Season with Tabasco sauce
and Cajun seasoning. Stir to mix well. Spoon into a lightly greased 2-quart baking
dish. Bake at 375 degrees for 45 minutes. Garnish with additional chopped green
onions and cooked peeled shrimp, if desired.

Serves 6

THE GREATEST PART OF OUR HAPPINESS DEPENDS ON
OUR DISPOSITIONS, NOT OUR CIRCUMSTANCES.

—*Martha Washington*

Oysters with Shrimp Dressing

1/2 loaf French bread, thinly sliced
3 pints unwashed shucked oysters
3 cups oyster liquor
1 cup (2 sticks) margarine
3 onions, finely chopped
1 bell pepper, finely chopped
1 rib celery, finely chopped
2 garlic cloves, minced
1 pound fresh deveined peeled
   medium shrimp
1 tablespoon salt

1 teaspoon black pepper
1 teaspoon white pepper
2 teaspoons cayenne pepper
2 teaspoons dried thyme, or
   1 tablespoon chopped fresh thyme
2 teaspoons dried basil, or
   1 tablespoon chopped fresh basil
6 drops of Tabasco sauce
1 cup sliced green onions
1 cup chopped fresh parsley
Grated Parmesan cheese

Arrange the bread in a single layer on a baking sheet. Bake at 200 degrees for up to 30 minutes to dry. Do not brown. Remove to a large bowl. Cover and chill 24 oysters. Cut the remaining oysters in half through the muscle. Pour the oyster liquor over the bread and let soak. Melt the butter in a heavy 4- to 6-quart saucepan over medium-high heat. Add the onions, bell pepper, celery and garlic. Cook for 45 minutes or until the vegetables are very soft, stirring occasionally. Add any extra oyster liquor you may have near the end of cooking and cook until evaporated. Cut the shrimp into thirds. Mix the salt, black pepper, white pepper and cayenne pepper in a small bowl. Remove and reserve 1 teaspoon. Add the remaining pepper mixture to the saucepan. Stir in the shrimp, thyme, basil and Tabasco sauce. Sauté over medium-high heat for 4 to 5 minutes or until the shrimp turn pink. Add the cut oysters and sauté just until the edges curl. Mix the soaked bread until well mashed. Add to the saucepan. Reduce the heat to low and cook until well mixed, stirring constantly. Remove from the heat. Stir in the green onions and parsley and let cool. Cover and chill for at least 2 hours. Place 24 cleaned oyster shells or 4-ounce ramekins on a baking sheet. Place 1 reserved oyster in each shell. Sprinkle with the reserved pepper mixture. Spoon the dressing into the shells, mounding slightly. Bake at 375 degrees for 25 to 30 minutes. Sprinkle generously with cheese and place under a broiler for 1 to 2 minutes.

Serves 10 to 12 as a first course or 6 as a main course

Shrimp Cakes with Jalapeño Tartar Sauce

1/2 cup bottled clam juice or water
1 1/2 pounds fresh deveined peeled shrimp
3 cups (or more) fresh bread crumbs
2 tablespoons unsalted butter
1 rib celery, finely chopped
8 green onions, chopped
1 teaspoon hot red pepper sauce

1 1/4 cups finely crushed saltine crackers
2 eggs, well beaten
1/3 cup mayonnaise
1/4 cup finely chopped fresh chives
Salt and pepper to taste
2 tablespoons (or more) unsalted butter
Jalapeño Tartar Sauce (below)

Bring the clam juice to a boil in a skillet. Add the shrimp and reduce the heat to low. Simmer, covered, for 1 minute. Stir the shrimp. Simmer, covered, until the shrimp turn pink. Drain and let cool. Chop the shrimp finely. Spread 3 cups bread crumbs in a shallow dish. Melt 2 tablespoons butter in a saucepan. Add the celery and green onions and sauté until the vegetables are tender. Remove from the heat and let cool to room temperature. Stir in the hot sauce, crackers, eggs, mayonnaise and chives. Season with salt and pepper. Stir in additional bread crumbs if the mixture is too wet. Shape into 12 patties. Coat the patties in the bread crumbs. Melt 2 tablespoons butter in a skillet. Add 1/2 the patties and fry until golden brown on both sides, turning once. Remove to a plate lined with paper towels and keep warm. Fry the remaining patties, adding more butter to the skillet if needed. Garnish with lemon wedges and chopped chives and serve with Jalapeño Tartar Sauce.

Serves 6

Jalapeño Tartar Sauce

1 cup mayonnaise
1 teaspoon Dijon mustard
2 teaspoons fresh lemon juice
1/4 cup finely chopped gherkins

1 jalapeño chile, seeded and finely chopped
Salt and pepper to taste

Combine the mayonnaise, Dijon mustard, lemon juice, gherkins and jalapeño in a bowl. Season with salt and pepper. Stir to mix well.

Seafood Eggplant Casserole Supreme

1 cup (2 sticks) butter
2 large eggplants, peeled and finely chopped
1/2 cup finely chopped onion
1/2 cup finely chopped celery
1/2 cup finely chopped green or red bell pepper
1 pound fresh deveined peeled medium shrimp
8 ounces claw crab meat
1/2 cup bread crumbs
Salt and pepper to taste
Garlic and other seasonings to taste (optional)

Melt the butter in a large saucepan. Add the eggplant, onion, celery and bell pepper. Cook over low heat for 30 minutes, stirring occasionally. Do not brown. Stir in the shrimp and crab meat. Cook for 10 minutes or until the shrimp turn pink, stirring occasionally. Remove from the heat and add the bread crumbs. Season with salt, pepper, garlic and other favorite seasonings. Stir to mix well. Spoon into a large casserole or individual ramekins. Bake at 350 degrees until golden brown. Serve immediately.

Serves 6

LIFE'S A JOURNEY, NOT A DESTINATION.

—Aerosmith

Meat, Poultry and Game

"A Joyful Noise"

C. Broussard
-2005-

One of my patients reported that the Blessed Mother had visited him three times. In addition, family members had witnessed a shadow cross his face. On one of the occasions, the patient was alone with his wife and dog in the room. The patient looked at the door and said, "Come in," yet when the wife looked no one was visible to her. The dog was also staring at the door. A few seconds later, the wife felt something that felt like a gown brush against her legs. At the same time she saw a shadow cross his face.

On numerous occasions after his passing, the wife as well as his daughter smelled a scent of roses in their home. On Father's Day, various family members were gathered for a barbeque. The patient's father was having a hard time dealing with his son's passing. During the gathering, a white feather came floating down and floated right into the father's hand. This was witnessed by the patient's wife and other family members.

—Dee Patin, R.N.

ARTIST: CHUCK BROUSSARD—"A JOYFUL NOISE"
Submitted in loving memory of Papop Camille, MomMom Ada Broussard, PawPaw Stewart &
MeMe Rozas upon whose foundation his art is crafted. He also dedicates this piece to Aunt Doris and
Uncle Perry with whom he shared a love of dark gravy and Day Lilies, Uncle Edward whom he admired
for painting his own car, and Uncle Bob who told him the difference between a banjo and a guitar.

Chuck's Cajun stock is a "thick as gumbo roux" and is reflected in the typical themes of his paintings. His paintings are known for their jewel-like tones and glazes, which are enhanced by a painterly Masters' style. His landscapes are often of rural South Louisiana and his figures of the people who live there.

Roast Beef

1 (3- to 4-pound) rump or sirloin roast
4 to 5 garlic cloves
1 to 2 teaspoons freshly ground pepper
Salt to taste
1 large onion, thickly sliced
1 (10-ounce) can beef broth
2 tablespoons cornstarch

Rinse the roast and pat dry. Stuff with the garlic and rub with the pepper and salt. Coat a large cast-iron saucepan or Dutch oven with nonstick cooking spray. Heat over high heat for 2 to 3 minutes. Add the roast and brown on all sides. Remove from the heat. Remove the roast to a plate and layer the onion in the bottom of the saucepan. Place the roast on the onions. Bake, covered, at 350 degrees for $2^{1}/_{2}$ to 3 hours. Remove the roast to a plate and cover. Mix the beef broth and cornstarch in a bowl. Pour into the saucepan. Bring to a boil and cook until thickened, stirring constantly. Season with salt and pepper. Serve with the roast.

Serves 8 to 10

I AM THE RESURRECTION AND THE LIFE: HE THAT BELIEVES

IN ME, THOUGH HE WERE DEAD, YET SHALL HE LIVE. AND WHOSOEVER

LIVES AND BELIEVES IN ME SHALL NEVER DIE.

—*John 11:25-26*

Grillades

¹/4 cup bacon drippings

4 pounds round steak, fat trimmed
  and steak cut into serving pieces

¹/2 cup all-purpose flour

¹/4 cup bacon drippings

1 cup chopped onion

2 cups chopped green onions

³/4 cup chopped celery

1¹/2 cups chopped green bell peppers

2 garlic cloves, minced

2 cups chopped tomatoes or tomatoes
  with green chiles

¹/2 teaspoon tarragon (optional)

²/3 teaspoon thyme

1 cup water

1 cup red wine

1 tablespoon salt

¹/2 teaspoon pepper

¹/2 teaspoon hot red pepper sauce

2 bay leaves

2 tablespoons Worcestershire sauce

3 tablespoons chopped fresh parsley

Hot cooked grits or rice

Heat ¹/4 cup bacon drippings in a large heavy saucepan. Add the meat and brown
on all sides. Remove the meat to a warm plate. Add the flour and ¹/4 cup bacon
drippings to the saucepan. Cook until dark brown, stirring constantly. Add the
onion, green onions, celery, bell peppers and garlic and sauté until the vegetables
are tender. Stir in the tomatoes, tarragon and thyme. Cook for 3 minutes. Stir in
the water and wine. Cook for several minutes, stirring constantly. Add the meat,
salt, pepper, hot sauce, bay leaves and Worcestershire sauce. Reduce the heat to low
and stir. Cook for 2 hours or until the meat is tender, stirring occasionally. Remove
from the heat and stir in the parsley. Remove the bay leaves. Cover and chill for
several hours or overnight. Reheat when ready to serve, adding more liquid if
needed. Serve over grits or rice.

Serves 8

Mustard Round Steak

2 to 3 pounds round steak, cut into $^1/_2$×3-inch strips
Salt and pepper to taste
Mustard
1 small jar dill pickles, drained and chopped
1 small onion, finely chopped
1 tablespoon chopped drained capers (optional)
1 cup all-purpose flour
Vegetable oil
Chopped onion

Arrange the meat strips on a work surface. Season with salt and pepper. Spread each strip with a small amount of mustard. Sprinkle evenly with the pickles, onion and capers. Roll up and secure with a wooden pick. Coat the meat rolls with the flour. Heat oil in the bottom of a large heavy saucepan. Add the meat rolls and brown on all sides. Stir in chopped onion and enough water to make a gravy. Simmer until the meat is cooked through.

Serves 4 to 6

I BELIEVE THAT IMAGINATION IS STRONGER THAN
KNOWLEDGE—MYTH IS MORE POTENT THAN HISTORY—
DREAMS ARE MORE POWERFUL THAN FACTS—HOPE
ALWAYS TRIUMPHS OVER EXPERIENCE—LAUGHTER IS THE
CURE FOR GRIEF—LOVE IS STRONGER THAN DEATH.

—*Robert Fulghum*

Lazy Man's Cabbage Rolls

1 head cabbage, chopped
1 large onion, chopped
1 large bell pepper, chopped
1 bunch green onion tops, chopped
1 to 2 tablespoons Creole seasoning or
*   salt and pepper to taste*
2 pounds ground beef
1 cup rice
1 (10-ounce) can tomatoes with green chiles
1 (12-ounce) can vegetable juice cocktail

Mix the cabbage, onion, bell pepper and 1/2 the green onion tops in a large bowl.
Stir in the Creole seasoning. Mix the ground beef, rice and remaining green onion
tops in a bowl. Place half the cabbage mixture in the bottom of a 10-cup rice
cooker. Top with the beef mixture. Pour the tomatoes with green chiles over the
meat layer. Top with the remaining cabbage mixture. Pour the vegetable juice
cocktail over the top. Cook, covered, for 30 to 45 minutes or until the meat is
cooked through.

Serves 6

LO, I AM WITH YOU ALWAYS, EVEN UNTO THE END OF TIME.

—Matthew 28:20

Leslie's Lasagna

2 pounds ground beef
1 large onion, chopped
1 large bell pepper, chopped
Salt and cayenne pepper to taste
2 jars sliced mushrooms, drained
3 cans tomato sauce
2 cans tomato paste
1 (10-ounce) can tomatoes with
    green chiles
1/2 teaspoon basil

1/2 teaspoon oregano
1/2 teaspoon dried parsley flakes
1 garlic clove, minced
3 cups water
1 package lasagna noodles,
    cooked al dente and drained
2 cups sour cream
1 to 2 cups (4 to 8 ounces) shredded
    mozzarella cheese

Brown the ground beef in a large saucepan with the onion and bell pepper, stirring until the ground beef is crumbly; drain. Season with salt and cayenne pepper. Stir in the mushrooms, tomato sauce, tomato paste, tomatoes with green chiles, basil, oregano, parsley, garlic and water. Cook over low heat for 20 minutes, stirring occasionally. Spread some of the tomato sauce in the bottom of a 9×13-inch baking dish or lasagna pan. Top with a 1/3 of the noodles and spread with some of the tomato sauce. Top with the sour cream. Add another 1/3 of the noodles and top with some of the tomato sauce. Add the remaining noodles and top with the remaining tomato sauce. Sprinkle with the cheese. Bake at 350 degrees for 1 hour.

Serves 10 to 12

Spaghetti and Meatballs

3 tablespoons olive oil
2 cups chopped onions
3 garlic cloves, minced
1/2 cup chopped celery
2 (6-ounce) cans tomato paste
2 (8-ounce) cans tomato sauce
3 quarts water
1/2 teaspoon salt
1/4 teaspoon pepper
1 tablespoon sugar

1 bay leaf
4 basil leaves or 1/4 cup chopped
   fresh basil
1 teaspoon anise seeds or fennel seeds
1 pinch of oregano
1 pinch of thyme
1/2 cup chopped fresh parsley
Meatballs (below)
Hot cooked spaghetti

Heat the olive oil in a large saucepan. Add the onions, garlic and celery and sauté until the vegetables are tender. Stir in the tomato paste and tomato sauce. Stir in the water, salt, pepper, sugar, bay leaf, basil, anise seeds, oregano, thyme and parsley. Cover the saucepan partially and bring to a boil. Reduce the heat to low. Simmer, partially covered, for 30 minutes, stirring often. Stir in the Meatballs. Cook, partially covered for 1 1/2 hours or until the sauce is thick and the meatballs are cooked through. Remove and discard the bay leaf. Serve over spaghetti.

Serves 12 to 16

Meatballs

2 pounds ground beef
2 pounds hot Italian sausage, casings
   removed
4 cups Italian-style seasoned bread
   crumbs
2 bunches green onions, chopped
1 cup chopped fresh parsley

12 garlic cloves, minced
1 cup (4 ounces) grated Romano cheese
4 eggs, beaten
2 tablespoons anise seeds
3 tablespoons salt
1 tablespoon pepper
Olive oil for frying

Mix the ground beef and sausage in a large bowl. Combine the bread crumbs, green onions, parsley, garlic, cheese, eggs, anise seeds, salt and pepper in a bowl. Stir to mix well. Add to the meat mixture. Stir to mix well. Shape into balls. Heat olive oil in a large skillet. Add the meatballs and brown on all sides.

Spaghetti Supreme

2 tablespoons olive oil
2 pounds lean ground beef
2 large yellow onions, chopped
1 green bell pepper, chopped
2 ribs celery, chopped
1 teaspoon minced fresh garlic
2 (14-ounce) cans whole tomatoes, crushed
1 (6-ounce) can tomato paste
2 cups water
1/4 cup dry red wine (optional)
2 bay leaves
Salt and cayenne pepper to taste
Oregano to taste
Basil to taste
8 ounces button mushrooms, stems removed and mushrooms sliced
1 (10-ounce) package spaghetti or angel hair pasta,
    cooked al dente, drained and kept warm
16 ounces Cheddar cheese, shredded
Grated Parmesan cheese

Heat the olive oil in a large heavy saucepan over medium heat. Add the ground beef and cook, stirring until the ground beef is crumbly; drain. Add the onions, bell pepper and celery and sauté for 5 to 8 minutes or until the vegetables are tender, stirring frequently. Add the garlic and sauté for 1 to 2 minutes. Stir in the tomatoes, tomato paste, water, wine and bay leaves. Season with salt, cayenne pepper, oregano and basil. Cook, partially covered, for 1 hour, stirring occasionally. Stir in the mushrooms and add more water, if needed. Cook for 10 minutes. Remove and discard the bay leaves. Spread some of the tomato sauce in the bottom of a large baking dish. Top with a layer of pasta and a layer of Cheddar cheese. Sprinkle with Parmesan cheese. Continue layering to use all of the tomato sauce, pasta, Cheddar cheese and Parmesan cheese. Bake at 350 degrees for 20 to 30 minutes or until the cheese is melted and light brown.

Serves 8 to 10

Hot Tamale Pie

1 1/2 pounds ground beef
1 large onion, chopped
2 garlic cloves, minced
1/2 bell pepper, chopped
1 (15-ounce) can tomato sauce
2 tablespoons chili powder
2 teaspoons cumin
Salt, black pepper and cayenne pepper to taste
6 cups water
2 cups yellow cornmeal
2 teaspoons chili powder
1 teaspoon cumin
Shredded Cheddar cheese

Brown the ground beef in a large saucepan, stirring until the meat is crumbly; drain. Add the onion, garlic and bell pepper and sauté until the vegetables are tender. Stir in the tomato sauce, 2 tablespoons chili powder and 2 teaspoons cumin. Season with salt, black pepper and cayenne pepper. Add enough water to make a thick sauce. Simmer, stirring occasionally. Spread in the bottom of a baking dish. Bring 6 cups water to a boil in a saucepan. Stir in the cornmeal slowly. Stir in 2 teaspoons chili powder and 1 teaspoon cumin. Season with salt and pepper. Reduce the heat to low. Cook for 10 to 15 minutes, stirring occasionally. Spread over the meat sauce in the baking dish. Sprinkle with cheese. Bake at 375 degrees for 30 minutes.

Serves 6 to 8

NOTE: You may add black beans, corn or chopped chiles to the tomato sauce mixture.

Lamb chops

Grated zest of 1 large lemon
3 tablespoons fresh lemon juice
1/4 cup olive oil
1 teaspoon salt
2 teaspoons Cajun seasoning
2 tablespoons dried thyme
2 tablespoons dried basil
1 onion, chopped
3 garlic cloves, minced
2 tablespoons Worcestershire sauce
1 bay leaf
10 lamb chops

Whisk the lemon zest, lemon juice, olive oil, salt, Cajun seasoning, thyme, basil, onion, garlic, Worcestershire sauce and bay leaf in a large bowl. Add the lamb chops and turn to coat. Cover and chill for 2 to 6 hours. Remove the chops and discard the marinade. Grill the chops over a hot fire for 4 to 5 minutes per side for medium-rare.

Serves 4

IF I TAKE THE WINGS OF THE MORNING AND SETTLE

AT THE FARTHEST LIMITS OF THE SEA, EVEN THERE YOUR HAND SHALL

LEAD ME, AND YOUR RIGHT HAND SHALL HOLD ME FAST.

—Psalms 139:9-10

Honey-Roasted Pork Tenderloin

1 (1¹/2-pound) pork tenderloin
Olive oil
Salt and black pepper to taste
Creole seasoning to taste
Lemon pepper to taste
Worcestershire sauce to taste
Soy sauce to taste
Pickapeppa Sauce to taste
Honey to taste
¹/2 cup white wine

Rub the tenderloins with olive oil. Season with salt, black pepper, Creole seasoning and lemon pepper to taste. Arrange the tenderloins in a baking pan. Drizzle with Worcestershire sauce, soy sauce, Pickapeppa Sauce and honey. Pour the wine into the bottom of the pan. Bake, uncovered, at 350 degrees for 45 minutes or until a meat thermometer inserted in the thickest part registers 165 degrees.

Serves 4 to 6

THE SPIRIT OF THE LORD SHALL REST UPON HIM, THE SPIRIT OF
WISDOM AND UNDERSTANDING, THE SPIRIT OF COUNSEL AND
MIGHT, THE SPIRIT OF KNOWLEDGE AND THE FEAR OF THE LORD.

—*Isaiah 11:2*

Cajun Pork Braid

1 pound ground pork
¹/2 cup chopped onion
¹/4 cup chopped celery
¹/4 cup chopped green bell pepper
1 garlic clove, minced
¹/2 teaspoon Cajun seasoning
Pepper to taste
8 ounces cream cheese, cubed
2 tablespoons chopped green onions
2 tablespoons chopped fresh parsley
1 teaspoon filé powder
1 (8-count) can refrigerator crescent rolls
1 egg, beaten

Brown the ground pork in a skillet over medium heat, stirring until the meat is crumbly; drain. Add the onion, celery, bell pepper, garlic and Cajun seasoning. Season with pepper. Cook over low heat for 5 minutes, stirring often. Add the cream cheese, green onions, parsley and filé powder. Cook until the cheese melts, stirring constantly. Unroll the crescent dough on a lightly greased baking sheet and press the seams to seal. Roll the dough with a lightly floured rolling pin to a 10×12-inch rectangle. Spoon the pork mixture down the center of the dough, leaving a 1-inch border at the ends and a 3-inch border on the sides. Cut the dough on the sides into ³/4-inch-wide diagonal strips. Brush the strips with some of the egg. Fold the strips diagonally over the filling, alternating sides, to form a braid. Brush with the remaining egg. Bake a 350 degrees for 25 minutes or until golden brown.

Serves 6 to 8

Barbecue Pork Ribs

2 cups packed brown sugar
1/2 cup coarse salt
1/4 cup paprika
1/4 cup dry mustard
2 teaspoons chili powder
2 teaspoons freshly ground black pepper
1 teaspoon garlic powder
1/4 teaspoon cayenne pepper
1 tablespoon oregano (optional)
2 to 3 large slabs pork ribs

Combine the brown sugar, salt, paprika, dry mustard, chili powder, black pepper, garlic powder, cayenne pepper and oregano in a bowl. Stir to mix well. Rinse the ribs and trim off excess fat, leaving some on for flavor. Pat dry with paper towels. Rub the brown sugar mixture into all sides of the ribs. Place on a large platter. Cover and chill overnight. Cook the ribs at 250 degrees in a smoker over indirect heat for 1 hour. Reduce the heat to 200 to 220 degrees and cook for 4 to 5 hours or until cooked through, rotating the ribs during cooking. Remove the ribs to a shallow baking pan and cover with foil. Bake at 100 to 120 degrees for 1 hour. Serve with all the fixings and good beer.

Serves 6

NOTE: You may add pecan, hickory or mesquite wood chips to the smoker the last hour of cooking. Use pecan wood chips to add sweetness and hickory or mesquite wood chips to provide a rich and flavorful taste. Oak wood chips may also be used during the last 20 to 30 minutes of smoking.

Penne with Mortadella and Cream

2 tablespoons butter
2 tablespoons olive oil
1 small onion, sliced
1 garlic clove, crushed
4 ounces mortadella or ham,
  cut into ¼-inch cubes
½ cup white wine
1 teaspoon cornstarch
3 tablespoons (or more) cold water
2 cups boiling chicken stock
12 ounces penne, cooked al dente
  and drained
1 cup heavy cream or milk
Grated Parmesan cheese
1 handful chopped parsley

Heat the butter and olive oil in a large saucepan. Add the onion and garlic and sauté until the onion is tender. Add the mortadella and sauté for a few minutes. Stir in the wine and cook until almost evaporated. Dissolve the cornstarch in the cold water in a small bowl. Add the cornstarch mixture and boiling chicken stock to the saucepan. Simmer until reduced to a creamy sauce, stirring constantly. Stir in the pasta and cream. Cook until heated through, stirring often. Remove from the heat and stir in cheese and the parsley. Serve immediately.

Serves 4

Rice Pot Jambalaya

1/2 cup (1 stick) butter or margarine, softened
1 pound smoked sausage, cut into pieces
1 small onion, finely chopped
1 small bell pepper, finely chopped
1 (10-ounce) can condensed French onion soup
1 (10-ounce) can beef broth
2 cups rice
1/2 cup water

Combine the butter, sausage, onion, bell pepper, onion soup, beef broth, rice and water in a bowl. Stir to mix well. Pour into a 5-cup rice cooker. Cook until the bell goes off. Stir and cover. Let stand for 15 to 20 minutes.

Serves 6

THE WORLD IS CHARGED WITH THE GRANDEUR OF GOD.

—Gerard Manley Hopkins

Sausage, Okra and Tomato Stew

1/4 cup olive oil

3 cups chopped okra

1 1/2 cups chopped onions

1 cup chopped bell pepper

1/2 cup chopped celery

1/2 cup chopped shallots

1 tablespoon minced garlic

6 large tomatoes, peeled, cored and mashed

1 1/2 cups water

1/2 cup ketchup

1 teaspoon oregano

1 teaspoon thyme

3 bay leaves

1 1/2 cups sliced smoked pork sausage

1 cup (1/2-inch pieces) tasso

1 tablespoon salt

1 tablespoon cayenne pepper

Hot cooked rice

Heat the olive oil in a skillet. Add the okra and sauté until all stickiness disappears. Remove from the heat. Sauté the onions, bell pepper, celery, shallots and garlic in a large nonstick saucepan until the vegetables are tender. Stir in the okra, tomatoes and water. Stir in the ketchup, oregano, thyme, bay leaves, sausage, tasso, salt and cayenne pepper. Cook for 1 to 1 1/2 hours over medium heat. Remove and discard the bay leaves. Serve over rice.

Serves 6 to 8

Smoked Sausage with Rice

12 ounces smoked country-style sausage links
1/2 cup water
1 (8-ounce) can unsweetened sliced pineapple
1 large onion, sliced
1 large green bell pepper, cut into 1-inch pieces
2 ribs celery, sliced
1 (14-ounce) can whole tomatoes, quartered
1 cup beef broth
1 tablespoon brown sugar
1/4 teaspoon garlic powder
1/4 teaspoon pepper
2 tablespoons cornstarch
4 cups hot cooked rice

Combine the sausage and water in a skillet. Cook, covered, for 5 minutes; drain. Slice the sausage thinly. Drain the pineapple, reserving the juice. Cut the pineapple into cubes. Combine the sausage, onion, bell pepper and celery in a large skillet. Sauté until the vegetables are tender-crisp. Stir in the pineapple, tomatoes, beef broth, brown sugar, garlic powder and pepper. Cover and simmer for 5 minutes. Mix the reserved pineapple juice and cornstarch in a small bowl. Add to the skillet. Cook for 2 minutes or until clear and thickened, stirring constantly. Serve over the rice.

Serves 4

Chicken Caprese with Tomato Basil Cream

2/3 cup soft bread crumbs
1/3 cup crumbled feta cheese
1 tablespoon chopped fresh basil, or 1 teaspoon dried basil
1/4 teaspoon salt
1/4 teaspoon pepper
3 tablespoons olive oil
2 tablespoons lemon juice
4 boneless skinless chicken breasts
Tomato-Basil Cream (below)

Mix the bread crumbs, cheese, basil, salt and pepper in a shallow dish. Whisk the olive oil and lemon juice in a shallow bowl until blended. Dip the chicken in the olive oil mixture. Dredge in the bread crumb mixture, pressing to coat. Place the chicken in a lightly greased 7×11-inch baking dish. Bake at 375 degrees for 30 minutes or until the chicken is cooked through. Serve with Tomato-Basil Cream.

Serves 4

Tomato Basil Cream

1 cup spaghetti sauce
2 tablespoons heavy cream, or light sour cream
1 tablespoon chopped fresh basil, or 1 teaspoon dried basil

Mix the spaghetti sauce, cream and basil in a small saucepan. Cook over low heat for 5 minutes or until heated through, stirring often.

crab-stuffed chicken

2 tablespoons butter or margarine
1/4 cup all-purpose flour
3/4 cup milk
3/4 cup chicken broth
1/3 cup chablis or other dry white wine
1 tablespoon butter
1/3 cup chopped green onions
1 pound white crab meat, drained and flaked
1 (4-ounce) can mushroom stems and pieces,
    drained and chopped
1/2 cup cracker crumbs
1 tablespoon chopped fresh parsley
1/4 teaspoon salt
1/2 teaspoon pepper
10 boneless skinless chicken breasts
1 cup shredded Swiss cheese
Paprika

Melt 2 tablespoons butter in a saucepan. Stir in the flour. Cook for a few minutes, stirring constantly. Mix the milk, chicken broth and wine in a bowl. Stir into the flour mixture gradually. Cook until thickened, stirring constantly. Remove from the heat. Melt 1 tablespoon butter in a large saucepan. Add the green onions and sauté until tender. Fold in the crab meat, mushrooms, cracker crumbs, parsley, salt and pepper. Stir in 2 tablespoons of the white sauce. Remove from the heat. Place the chicken on a work surface. Flatten to 1/4-inch with a meat mallet. Spoon the crab mixture onto the center of each chicken breast. Fold the ends over and place seam side down in a greased baking dish. Pour the remaining white sauce over the chicken. Bake, covered, at 350 degrees for 1 hour or until the chicken is cooked through. Sprinkle with the cheese and paprika. Bake, uncovered, for 1 minute longer or until the cheese melts.

Serves 10

Chicken Divine

Vegetable oil or olive oil
12 boneless skinless chicken breasts
2 (10-ounce) cans condensed cream of chicken soup
1 (10-ounce) can condensed cream of mushroom soup
1 cup sour cream
¹/₂ cup white wine
2 (2-ounce) cans French-fried onions

Heat a small amount of oil in a large skillet. Add the chicken and brown on both sides. Remove to a large baking dish. Remove any excess drippings from the skillet. Stir in the chicken soup, mushroom soup, sour cream, wine and 1 can French-fried onions. Heat until bubbly, stirring often. Pour over the chicken. Bake, covered, at 350 degrees for 1 hour. Sprinkle with the remaining can of French-fried onions. Bake, uncovered, for 15 minutes longer or until golden brown and the chicken is cooked through.

Serves 10 to 12

NOTHING IN LIFE IS MORE WONDERFUL THAN FAITH—THE ONE GREAT MOVING FORCE WHICH WE CAN NEITHER WEIGH IN THE BALANCE NOR TEST IN THE CRUCIBLE.

—*Sir William Osler*

Lemon Chicken with Potatoes

¹/4 cup vegetable oil
1 large onion, chopped
5 or 6 garlic cloves, chopped
6 to 8 potatoes, peeled and cut into large cubes
2 to 3 pounds boneless chicken breasts,
    cut into large cubes
3 cups water
Salt and pepper to taste
Allspice to taste
Cinnamon to taste (optional)
Juice of 2 or 3 lemons

Heat the oil in a large saucepan. Add the onion and garlic and sauté until the onions are tender. Remove to a bowl with a slotted spoon. Add the potatoes and sauté until browned on all sides. Remove to a bowl with a slotted spoon. Add the chicken and sauté until browned on all sides. Return the onions, garlic and potatoes to the saucepan. Stir in the water. Season with salt, pepper, allspice and cinnamon. Bring to a boil and reduce the heat to medium. Simmer for 30 minutes, stirring occasionally. Remove from the heat and stir in the lemon juice. Let stand, covered, for 10 minutes.

Serves 4 to 6

Knock-Your-Socks-Off Chicken Parmesan

8 skinless chicken thighs
1 package Shake'n Bake for pork
1 (10-ounce) can condensed
  cream of chicken soup
1 (10-ounce) can condensed
  cream of mushroom soup
1 large jar pizza sauce
1 teaspoon dried parsley flakes
1 teaspoon oregano
8 ounces sliced provolone cheese
Hot cooked angel hair pasta
Grated Parmesan or Romano cheese

Add 4 chicken thighs to 1 envelope of the Shake'n Bake in the bag provided. Shake to coat the chicken. Remove the chicken to a 9×13-inch baking dish coated with nonstick cooking spray. Repeat with the remaining chicken and Shake'n Bake and place in the baking dish. Bake at 350 degrees for 30 minutes or until golden brown. Mix the chicken soup, mushroom soup, pizza sauce, parsley and oregano in a bowl. Spoon half of the sauce over the chicken. Arrange the provolone cheese on top. Pour the remaining sauce over the cheese. Cover with foil. Bake at 350 degrees for 20 minutes. Uncover and bake for 10 minutes longer or until the top is light brown and the chicken is cooked through. Serve over angel hair pasta and sprinkle with Parmesan cheese.

Serves 4 to 6

sherried stewed chicken

1 (2¹/2-pound) chicken, cut up
¹/2 cup Bisquick
¹/2 cup (1 stick) margarine
2 tablespoons shortening
2¹/2 cups water
¹/2 cup cream sherry
3 carrots, sliced
¹/2 cup sliced celery
2 green onions, chopped
2 bay leaves
2 tablespoons grated Parmesan cheese
1 teaspoon dried parsley flakes
Salt and pepper to taste
Hot cooked rice or hot mashed cooked potatoes

Rinse the chicken and pat dry. Dredge in the Bisquick to coat. Melt the margarine and shortening in a Dutch oven. Add the chicken and brown on all sides. Remove the chicken to a large plate. Combine the water, sherry, carrots, celery, green onions, bay leaves, cheese and parsley in a Dutch oven. Season with salt and pepper. Stir to mix well, scraping any browned bits from the bottom of the pan. Add the chicken, placing the larger pieces on the bottom. Bring to a boil and reduce the heat. Simmer, covered, for 1 hour or until the chicken is cooked through. Remove and discard the bay leaves. Remove the chicken to a platter. Chop the chicken, discarding the bones. Cover and chill. Chill the Dutch oven until the fat rises. Remove the surface fat. Return the chicken to the Dutch oven. Cook until heated through. Serve over rice or mashed potatoes.

Serves 4 to 6

chicken Broccoli Rice casserole

1/4 cup (1/2 stick) butter or
   margarine
1 large onion, chopped
1 (10-ounce) can condensed cream
   of chicken soup
8 ounces Velveeta cheese, cubed
1 (5-ounce) can evaporated milk
2 cups sliced mushrooms

2 (10-ounce) packages frozen chopped
   broccoli
1 cup uncooked rice, cooked
1 chicken, cooked, boned and cut into
   small chunks
1/4 cup slivered almonds
Salt and pepper to taste

Melt the butter in a large saucepan. Add the onion and sauté until tender. Stir in the soup, cheese, evaporated milk, mushrooms and broccoli. Cook until the cheese melts and the broccoli is heated through, stirring often. Stir in the rice, chicken and almonds. Season with salt and pepper. Pour into a large casserole. Bake at 325 degrees for 1 hour.

Serves 12

cajun chicken Stew

1/2 cup vegetable oil
1 chicken, cut up
3/4 cup all-purpose flour
1 bunch green onions, chopped
1 green bell pepper, chopped

1 bunch parsley, chopped
1/4 teaspoon salt
1/4 teaspoon pepper
1/4 teaspoon hot red pepper sauce
Hot cooked rice

Heat the oil in a Dutch oven. Add the chicken and brown on all sides. Remove the chicken to a plate. Add the flour to the Dutch oven. Cook until dark brown, stirring constantly. Stir in the green onions, bell pepper and parsley. Cook for a few minutes, stirring constantly, adding a small amount of oil if the mixture is too stiff to stir. Add the chicken. Add enough water to barely cover the chicken. Stir in the salt, pepper and hot sauce. Cook, covered, until the chicken is almost falling off the bones. Serve over rice.

Serves 8

Enchiladas Monterey

1 to 2 tablespoons vegetable oil
1 tablespoon chopped onion
1 pound chopped cooked chicken
Salt and pepper to taste
4 ounces cream cheese, softened
1/2 to 3/4 cup sour cream

1 tablespoon chopped jalapeño chiles or
   canned green chiles
12 flour tortillas
Monterey Sauce (below)
8 ounces shredded Monterey Jack cheese

Heat the oil in a skillet. Add the onion and sauté until tender. Add the chicken and season with salt and pepper. Cook for a few minutes, stirring constantly. Remove from the heat. Beat the cream cheese and sour cream in a large bowl until creamy. Add the chicken mixture and jalapeño chiles and season with salt and pepper. Stir to mix well. Soften the tortillas in the microwave or dip in hot oil and arrange on a work surface. Spoon the chicken mixture down the center of each tortilla and roll up. Place in a large shallow baking dish or individual baking dishes. Cover with Monterey Sauce and sprinkle with the Monterey Jack cheese. Bake at 350 degrees until the cheese is melted and bubbly.

Serves 6

Monterey Sauce

3/4 cup (1 1/2 sticks) butter
3/4 cup all-purpose flour
4 cups rich chicken stock, warmed
3/4 cup half-and-half, warmed
1 tablespoon chopped pimento

1 tablespoon chopped green chiles
1 tablespoon chopped cilantro
2 teaspoons salt
1/4 teaspoon white pepper

Melt the butter in a saucepan over low heat. Stir in the flour gradually. Cook for a few minutes, stirring constantly. Do not brown. Remove from the heat and stir in the chicken stock. Cook over low heat until thickened and smooth, stirring constantly. Stir in the half-and-half. Stir in the pimentos, green chiles, cilantro, salt and pepper. Cook for a few minutes, stirring constantly. Do not let boil. Keep warm.

chicken Enchiladas

2 tablespoons butter
1 onion, chopped
2 cups seasoned chopped cooked chicken
8 ounces cream cheese
1¹/2 (4-ounce) cans chopped green chiles
Salt and pepper to taste
Canned chicken broth or chicken broth
*   from cooked chicken*
Small or large flour tortillas
1 cup (4 ounces) shredded Monterey Jack cheese
¹/2 cup half-and-half or milk

Melt the butter in a saucepan. Add the onion and sauté until tender. Stir in the chicken, cream cheese and green chiles. Season with salt and pepper. Stir in a small amount of chicken broth. Cook until the cheese melts, stirring often. Remove from the heat. Spoon the chicken mixture down the center of each tortilla and roll up. Place seam side down in a greased baking dish. Sprinkle with the Monterey Jack cheese and drizzle with the half-and-half. Cover with foil. Bake at 325 degrees for 45 minutes or until bubbly.

Serves 8

SO LONG AS WE LOVE WE SERVE; SO LONG AS WE ARE LOVED

BY OTHERS, I WOULD ALMOST SAY THAT WE ARE INDISPENSABLE; AND

NO MAN IS USELESS WHILE HE HAS A FRIEND.

—*Robert Louis Stevenson*

chicken pie

2 unbaked deep-dish pie shells
2 whole chicken breasts, cooked,
   boned and diced
3 hard-cooked eggs, chopped
1 cup chopped celery
1 cup chopped onion
1 (8-ounce) can water chestnuts,
   drained and diced
^{1}/2 cup mayonnaise
1 (10-ounce) can condensed
   cream of chicken soup
Juice of ^{1}/2 lemon
Salt and pepper to taste
1 cup shredded cheese
1 (5-ounce) package potato chips, crushed

Prick the pie shells with a fork. Bake at 350 degrees for 10 minutes. Remove to a wire rack. Combine the chicken, eggs, celery, onion, water chestnuts, mayonnaise, soup and lemon juice in a large bowl. Season with salt and pepper. Stir to mix well. Spoon into the pie shells. Sprinkle with the cheese and top with the crushed potato chips. Bake at 350 degrees for 30 minutes.

Serves 12

chicken Turnovers

10 chicken breasts, cooked and chopped
8 ounces cream cheese, softened
1 (4-ounce) can sliced mushrooms, drained
1/2 teaspoon lemon pepper
3 (8-count) cans refrigerator crescent rolls
1 cup herb-seasoned stuffing mix
1/2 cup pecan pieces
2/3 cup apricot preserves
1/3 cup yellow mustard

Combine the chicken, cream cheese, mushrooms and lemon pepper in a bowl. Stir to mix well. Unroll the crescent dough on a work surface. Press the seams between 2 rolls to seal, making 12 rectangles. Place a ball of the chicken mixture in the center of each rectangle. Bring the sides of the dough together to cover the chicken. Pinch the edges to seal. Mix the stuffing mix and pecans in a shallow dish. Press the top of the turnovers into the stuffing mixture to coat. Place crumb side up on a nonstick baking sheet. Bake at 350 degrees for 20 to 30 minutes. Mix the preserves and mustard in a small saucepan. Cook until heated through, stirring often. Serve warm over the turnovers.

Serves 12

WE HAVE NO MORE RIGHT TO CONSUME HAPPINESS WITHOUT
PRODUCING IT THAN TO CONSUME WEALTH WITHOUT PRODUCING IT.

—*George Bernard Shaw*

Fried Turkey

1 (14- to 18-pound) turkey, thawed, giblets removed
1/4 cup soy sauce
1/4 cup teriyaki sauce
1/4 cup liquid crab boil
1/4 cup paprika
1/4 cup Creole seasoning
4 to 5 gallons peanut or vegetable oil

Rinse the turkey and pat dry. Mix the soy sauce, teriyaki sauce and crab boil in a measuring cup. Pour into a poultry injector. Inject the turkey in various places with the soy sauce mixture. Mix the paprika and Creole seasoning in a small bowl. Rub into the skin of the turkey. Place the turkey in a large sealable plastic and seal the bag. Chill for 12 to 24 hours. Heat the oil in a turkey fryer to 350 degrees. Place the turkey in the frying basket and carefully lower into the oil. Cook for 4 minutes per pound or until the turkey is cooked through. Remove the turkey to a serving platter and let stand for 10 to 15 minutes.

Serves 8 to 14

NOTE: This must be cooked outdoors.

SHALL WE MAKE A NEW RULE OF LIFE FROM TONIGHT: ALWAYS TO

TRY TO BE A LITTLE KINDER THAN IS NECESSARY?

—James M. Barrie

Drunken Duck

2 large onions, chopped
2 large garlic cloves, chopped
1 bell pepper, chopped
4 ribs celery, chopped
Chopped green onion tops
Chopped fresh parsley
2 large ducks, or 4 teal
Salt and pepper to taste
1 box chicken-fry mix
$^1/_2$ cup vegetable oil
1 (10-ounce) can beer

Place the onions, garlic, bell pepper, celery, green onions and parsley in the bottom of a large saucepan. Season the ducks with salt and pepper and coat in the chicken-fry mix. Heat the oil in a large skillet. Add the ducks and brown on all sides. Place the ducks on the vegetables in the saucepan. Pour the beer over the top. Simmer for 1$^1/_2$ hours or until the ducks are tender and cooked through.

Serves 4 to 8

BE PATIENT TOWARD ALL THAT IS UNRESOLVED IN YOUR HEART
AND TRY TO LIVE THE QUESTIONS THEMSELVES LIKE LOCKED DOORS
AND LIKE BOOKS THAT ARE WRITTEN IN A FOREIGN LANGUAGE.

—Rainer Maria Rilke

Pan-Roasted Quail

10 to 12 quail (approximately 12 weeks old)
Cajun seasoning
2 or 3 onions, chopped
2 green bell peppers, chopped
3 ribs celery, chopped
Vegetable oil
1 cup red wine
1 can mushrooms
Tony Chachere's gravy mix
Hot cooked white rice or wild rice

Season the quail inside and out with Cajun seasoning. Mix the onions, bell peppers and celery in a bowl. Stuff into the bird cavities. Heat enough oil to coat the bottom of a roaster. Add the quail and brown on all sides. Add enough water to barely cover the birds. Cook, covered, over low heat for 1 to 1^1/$_2$ hours. Stir in the wine and mushrooms, Cook, uncovered, for 30 minutes. Stir in gravy mix to thicken. Serve over rice.

Serves 5 or 6

IT ISN'T WHAT YOU HAVE, OR WHO YOU ARE, OR WHERE
YOU ARE, OR WHAT YOU ARE DOING THAT MAKES YOU HAPPY
OR UNHAPPY. IT IS WHAT YOU THINK ABOUT IT.

—*Dale Carnegie*

Smothered Quail

1/2 cup olive oil
8 dressed quail
1/2 cup chopped onion
1/2 cup chopped bell pepper
1/2 cup chopped celery
1/3 cup chopped fresh parsley
1/4 cup Tony Chachere's brown gravy mix
2 cups water
1 teaspoon salt
1 teaspoon cayenne pepper
1 teaspoon Kitchen Bouquet
1/4 teaspoon oregano
1/4 teaspoon thyme
3 bay leaves
Pinch of sugar
Tabasco sauce to taste

Heat the olive oil in a large heavy saucepan. Add the quail and brown on all sides. Remove the quail to a plate. Add the onion, bell pepper, celery and parsley to the saucepan. Sauté until the vegetables are tender. Combine the gravy mix and water in a saucepan. Bring to a boil, stirring constantly. Add to the vegetables. Stir in the salt, cayenne pepper, Kitchen Bouquet, oregano, thyme, bay leaves and sugar. Add the quail. Season with Tabasco sauce. Cook over medium heat for 1 to 1 1/2 hours or until the quail are tender and cooked through. Remove and discard the bay leaves.

Serves 4

Rabbit Sauce Piquant

1 (1- to 2-pound) rabbit, cut into 8 pieces
Cajun seasoning
2/3 cup olive oil
2/3 cup chopped onion
2/3 cup chopped bell pepper
1/2 cup chopped shallots
1/2 cup chopped celery
1 tablespoon chopped garlic
1/4 cup Tony Chachere's brown gravy mix
2 cups water
1 tablespoon Kitchen Bouquet
1 teaspoon tomato paste
1 teaspoon oregano
1 teaspoon thyme
Pinch of sugar
Tabasco Sauce to taste
Hot cooked rice

Coat the rabbit with Cajun seasoning. Cover and chill overnight. Heat the olive oil in a large heavy saucepan. Add the rabbit and brown on all sides. Remove the rabbit to a plate. Add the onion, bell pepper, shallots, celery and garlic to the saucepan. Sauté until the vegetables are tender. Combine the gravy mix and water in a saucepan. Bring to a boil, stirring constantly. Add to the vegetables. Stir in the Kitchen Bouquet, tomato paste, oregano, thyme and sugar. Add the rabbit. Cook over medium heat until the rabbit is tender and cooked through. Season with Tabasco sauce. Serve over rice.

Serves 4

Desserts

Four years ago, my brother Robert and his wife Sherry experienced the heartbreak of a still birth. A year later, though, Sherry gave birth to a healthy little girl whom she and Robert named Haley.

The following year, there was a miscarriage. When Haley was two, another baby girl was born; her name was Cassie. Tragedy visited the couple again, though, when Cassie died suddenly at the age of six months.

About two months after Cassie's death, Haley was at home with her babysitter. The two of them were swinging on a swing suspended from a sturdy oak branch. For some unknown reason, the branch snapped and came crashing down around Haley and the babysitter. Neither one was injured, but they were trapped by the limbs of the mammoth tree branch. Luckily, the babysitter had a cell phone handy and called on neighbors to rescue them.

Later, when recounting the incident to her mother, Haley, stated matter-of-factly, "You know, Cassie pushed me out of the way."

We believe in angels.

—Lynn Darby, R.Ph.

**ARTIST: BONNIE CAMOS—"EVER WONDER WHY
YOUR DESSERTS TASTE SO SWEET?"**
Submitted in memory of: son, Nicholas, mother, Doris, Aunt Coonie

Bonnie has been a working artist in Lafayette for 20 years. When asked to do this project, she had thoughts of little angels in the kitchen while remembering the death of her infant son, Nicholas. Hospice of Acadiana is privileged to have some of Bonnie's work displayed in the extensive art collection housed in its building.

Almond Bundt Cake

3 cups all-purpose flour
1 teaspoon salt
1/2 teaspoon baking powder
1 cup milk
1 teaspoon rum extract
1 teaspoon coconut extract
1 1/2 cups shortening
2 2/3 cups sugar
5 eggs
Glaze (below)

Mix the flour, salt and baking powder together. Mix the milk, rum extract and coconut extract together in a small bowl. Beat the shortening and sugar in a large bowl until light and fluffy. Add the eggs, 1 at a time, beating well after each addition. Beat in the dry ingredients alternately with the milk mixture. Pour into a greased bundt pan. Bake at 325 degrees for 1 hour or until a wooden pick inserted in the center comes out clean. Let cool in the pan for 15 minutes. Invert onto a serving plate. Poke holes in the warm cake with a wooden pick. Pour the Glaze slowly over the warm cake.

Serves 12 to 16

Glaze

1 cup sugar
1/2 cup water
1 teaspoon almond extract

Mix the sugar, water and almond extract in a small saucepan. Bring to a boil over medium heat, stirring occasionally.

Red Delicious Apple Cake

3 cups sifted all-purpose flour
2 teaspoons ground cinnamon
1¹/2 teaspoons baking soda
1 teaspoon salt
1 cup vegetable oil
2 cups sugar
2 eggs
1 tablespoon vanilla extract
1 cup chopped pecans or walnuts
¹/2 cup milk
3 cups chopped peeled Red Delicious apples

Mix the flour, cinnamon, baking soda and salt together. Beat the oil, sugar, eggs and vanilla in a large bowl. Fold in the dry ingredients. Stir in the pecans. Stir in the milk. Stir in the apples. Pour into a greased and floured bundt pan. Bake at 350 degrees for 1 hour and 10 minutes or until a wooden pick inserted in the center comes out clean. Let cool in the pan for 15 minutes. Remove to a wire rack to cool.

Serves 12

GRACE STRIKES US WHEN WE ARE IN GREAT PAIN AND RESTLESSNESS. . .SOMETIMES AT THAT MOMENT A WAVE OF LIGHT BREAKS INTO OUR DARKNESS, AND IT IS AS THOUGH A VOICE WERE SAYING: "YOU ARE ACCEPTED."

—*Paul Tillich*

Banana Bundt Cake

2^1/2 cups all-purpose flour
2^1/2 teaspoons baking powder
Pinch of salt
1 cup buttermilk
1 teaspoon baking soda
3 ripe bananas, mashed
2 cups sugar
2 eggs
1 cup melted shortening, or
    ^{1}/2 cup (1 stick) butter, melted
1 teaspoon vanilla extract

Sift the flour, baking powder and salt together. Mix the buttermilk and baking soda in a small bowl. Beat the bananas and sugar in a large bowl. Beat in the eggs. Beat in the buttermilk mixture, shortening and vanilla. Beat in the dry ingredients. Pour into a greased and floured bundt pan. Bake at 350 degrees for 40 minutes or until a wooden pick inserted in the center comes out clean. Let cool in the pan for 15 minutes. Remove to a wire rack to cool.

Serves 12 to 16

THE GENIUS OF CHRISTIANITY IS TO HAVE PROCLAIMED THAT THE
PATH TO THE DEEPEST MYSTERY IS THE PATH OF LOVE.

—*André Malraux*

Jam Cake

4 cups all-purpose flour
1 teaspoon each ground allspice and ground cloves
1/2 cup buttermilk
1 teaspoon baking soda
1 cup (2 sticks) softened butter or shortening
2 cups sugar
6 egg yolks
1 cup blackberry jam with seeds
6 eggs whites, stiffly beaten
Filling (below)

Sift the flour, allspice and cloves together. Mix the buttermilk and baking soda together in a small bowl. Beat the butter and sugar in a large bowl. Add the egg yolks, 1 at a time, beating well after each addition. Beat in the jam. Beat in the dry ingredients alternately with the buttermilk mixture. Fold in the egg whites. Pour into 4 greased and floured cake pans. Bake at 350 degrees for 50 to 55 minutes or until a wooden pick inserted in the center comes out clean. Cool in the pans for 10 minutes. Remove to a wire rack to cool completely. Spread the Filling between the layers and over the top and side of the cake.

Serves 12

Filling

3 cups sugar
1/2 cup (1 stick) butter
1 cup milk
1 cup each raisins and chopped nuts
1 teaspoon vanilla extract

Mix the sugar, butter, milk and raisins in a saucepan. Cook to 234 degrees on a candy thermometer, soft-ball stage. Remove from the heat and add the nuts and vanilla. Beat to a spreading consistency. Add a small amount of evaporated milk if the mixture becomes sugary when beating.

Better-Than-Almost-Anything Cake

1 (2-layer) package German Chocolate
    cake mix, batter prepared according
    to the package directions
1 (14-ounce) can sweetened condensed milk
1 (16- to 17-ounce) jar caramel, butterscotch or
    fudge ice cream topping
1 (8-ounce) container frozen whipped
    topping, thawed
1 (8-ounce) package toffee chips or toffee bits

Pour the batter into a greased 9×13-inch cake pan. Bake according to the package directions. Cool in the pan for 15 minutes. Poke holes every $1/2$-inch in the top of the cake with the handle of a wooden spoon. Drizzle the sweetened condensed milk evenly over the warm cake. Let stand until absorbed. Drizzle the caramel topping over the cake. Loosen the cake from the side of the pan with a sharp knife. Cover and chill for at least 2 hours. Spread the whipped topping over the cake and sprinkle with the toffee chips. Cover and chill until ready to serve.

Serves 15

YOU GAIN STRENGTH, COURAGE AND CONFIDENCE BY EVERY
EXPERIENCE IN WHICH YOU REALLY STOP TO LOOK FEAR IN THE FACE.

—*Eleanor Roosevelt*

chocolate sheet cake

2 cups all-purpose flour
2 cups sugar
1 cup (2 sticks) margarine
1/3 cup baking cocoa
1 cup water
1/2 cup buttermilk
1 teaspoon baking soda
1/2 teaspoon vanilla extract
2 eggs, beaten
Frosting (below)

Mix the flour and sugar in a large bowl. Melt the margarine in a saucepan. Stir in the baking cocoa and water. Bring to a boil, stirring occasionally. Add to the flour mixture. Stir in the buttermilk, baking soda and vanilla. Add the eggs and stir to mix well. Pour into a nonstick 11×16-inch baking pan. Bake at 400 degrees for 20 minutes or until a wooden pick inserted in the center comes out clean. Remove to a wire rack to cool slightly. Pour the warm Frosting evenly over the warm cake. Let cool before serving.

Serves 20

Frosting

1/2 cup (1 stick) margarine
6 tablespoons milk
2 heaping tablespoons baking cocoa
1 (16-ounce) package confectioners' sugar
1 cup chopped pecans
1 teaspoon vanilla extract

Combine the margarine, milk and baking cocoa in a saucepan. Bring to a boil, stirring often. Remove from the heat and stir in the confectioners' sugar, pecans and vanilla.

Fig Cake

1 cup shortening
1 cup sugar
2 eggs
1/2 small bottle vanilla extract
2 cups fig preserves
1 cup milk

2 teaspoons baking soda
2 teaspoons ground cinnamon
2 cups all-purpose flour
1 cup pecans
1 cup raisins

Beat the shortening and sugar in a large bowl. Beat in the eggs and vanilla. Stir in the fig preserves and milk. Add the baking soda, cinnamon, flour, pecans and raisins and stir to mix well. Pour into a greased 9×13-inch baking pan. Bake at 350 degrees for 1 hour and 20 minutes or until a wooden pick inserted in the center comes out clean. Remove to a wire rack to cool.

Serves 15

Mandarin Orange Cake

1 (2-layer) package yellow cake mix
4 eggs
1/2 cup (1 stick) butter, softened
2 (11-ounce) cans mandarin oranges,
   drained and juice reserved

1 (20-ounce) can crushed pineapple
1 large package vanilla instant
   pudding mix
1 (8-ounce) container frozen whipped
   topping, thawed

Combine the cake mix, eggs, butter and reserved juice in a large bowl. Beat with an electric mixer until well mixed. Fold in the oranges. Pour into 2 greased and floured 8-inch cake pans. Bake at 350 degrees for 30 to 40 minutes or until the cake pulls away from the side of the pan. (The cake will not rise much.) Cool in the pans for 10 minutes. Remove to a wire rack to cool completely. Mix the pineapple and pudding mix in a bowl. Fold in the whipped topping. Spread between the layers and over the top and side of the cake. Chill until ready to serve.

Serves 12

strawberry cake

1 (2-layer) package white cake mix
1 tablespoon all-purpose flour
1 (3-ounce) package strawberry gelatin
3/4 cup vegetable oil
1/2 cup water
1/2 cup frozen strawberries,
    thawed and mashed
4 eggs
Icing (below)

Mix the cake mix, flour and gelatin in a large bowl. Beat in the oil, water and strawberries. Add the eggs, 1 at a time, beating well after each addition. Pour into a nonstick 9×13-inch baking pan. Bake at 350 degrees for 25 to 30 minutes or until a wooden pick inserted in the center comes out clean. Remove to a wire rack to cool completely. Spread the Icing over the cooled cake.

Serves 6 to 8

Icing

2 tablespoons margarine, softened
1/2 cup frozen strawberries,
    thawed and mashed
2 1/2 cups confectioners' sugar

Beat the margarine, strawberries and confectioners' sugar in a bowl to mix well.

watergate cake

1 (2-layer) package white cake mix
1 (3-ounce) package pistachio
   pudding mix
3 eggs
1 cup vegetable oil
1 cup lemon-lime soda

1/2 cup walnuts
2 envelopes Dream Whip topping mix
1 (3-ounce) package pistachio
   pudding mix
1 1/2 cups milk
1/2 cup walnuts

Combine the cake mix, 1 package pudding mix, the eggs, oil and soda in a large bowl. Beat with an electric mixer for 1 1/2 to 2 minutes. Stir in 1/2 cup walnuts. Pour into 3 greased cake pans. Bake at 350 degrees for 20 to 30 minutes or until a wooden pick inserted in the center comes out clean. Cool in the pans for 10 minutes. Remove to a wire rack to cool completely. Combine the topping mix, 1 package pudding mix and the milk in a bowl. Stir to mix well. Stir in 1/2 cup walnuts. Spread between the layers and over the top and side of the cake. Chill until ready to serve.

Serves 6 to 8

Blueberry Cream Pie

1 cup sugar
1 large container frozen whipped
   topping, thawed
8 ounces cream cheese, softened

2 baked (9-inch) pie shells
4 bananas, thickly sliced
1 (21-ounce) can blueberry pie filling

Mix the sugar and whipped topping in a bowl. Add the cream cheese and stir to mix well. Arrange the banana slices in the bottom of the pie shells. Spread with the cream cheese mixture. Spread 1/2 can pie filling over the top of each pie. Cover and chill until firm.

Serves 12

Blueberry and White Chocolate Cheese Pie

1 cup roasted ground pecans
1/2 cup packed brown sugar
1/4 cup (1/2 stick) butter, melted
4 ounces white chocolate, grated
8 ounces cream cheese, softened
1/4 cup sour cream
2 cups fresh blueberries
1/4 cup granulated sugar

Mix the pecans, brown sugar and butter in a bowl. Press into the bottom and slightly up the sides of a 9-inch tart pan lined with parchment paper. Chill until firm. Melt the chocolate in the top of a double boiler over hot water, stirring constantly. Beat the cream cheese in a bowl with an electric mixer for 3 minutes. Add the melted chocolate and beat for 1 minute. Add the sour cream and beat until very smooth. Spoon into a pastry bag fitted with a star tip. Pipe into the prepared crust in concentric circles, starting in the center. Chill until firm. Combine the blueberries and granulated sugar in a bowl. Toss gently to coat. Spoon over the top of the pie. Garnish with white chocolate shavings and lemon zest.

Serves 6 to 8

THOSE WHO LOVE DEEPLY NEVER GROW OLD; THEY MAY DIE

OF OLD AGE, BUT THEY DIE YOUNG.

—Arthur Wing Pinero

chocolate Fudge Pie

3 eggs
1 cup sugar
1/2 cup (1 stick) butter, melted
1/3 cup baking cocoa
1/4 cup all-purpose flour
1/8 teaspoon salt
1 teaspoon vanilla extract
3/4 cup chopped pecans

Whisk the eggs and sugar in a large bowl. Add the butter, baking cocoa, flour, salt and vanilla. Stir to mix well. Stir in the pecans. Pour into a lightly greased 9-inch pie plate. Bake at 350 degrees for 25 to 30 minutes. Remove to a wire rack to cool.

Serves 6 to 8

NOTE: The pie will be puffed when removed from the oven but will fall as it cools.

I DO NOT SEEK TO UNDERSTAND IN ORDER TO BELIEVE,
BUT I BELIEVE IN ORDER TO UNDERSTAND. FOR I BELIEVE THIS:
UNLESS I BELIEVE, I WILL NOT UNDERSTAND.

—*Saint Anselm*

Coconut Cream Pie

4 egg yolks
2/3 cup sugar
1/2 teaspoon salt
2 1/2 tablespoons cornstarch
2 cups milk
1 tablespoon butter
3/4 cup flaked coconut
1 baked (9-inch) pie shell
4 egg whites
1/4 teaspoon cream of tartar
1/2 cup sugar
Flaked coconut

Mix the egg yolks, 2/3 cup sugar, the salt, cornstarch, milk and butter in a saucepan. Cook until thickened, stirring constantly. Stir in 3/4 cup coconut. Pour into the pie shell. Combine the egg whites, cream of tartar and 1/2 cup sugar in a bowl. Beat until stiff peaks form. Spread over the filling, sealing to the edge. Sprinkle with coconut. Bake at 350 degrees for 15 minutes or until golden brown and the egg white is cooked through. Remove to a wire rack to cool.

Serves 6 to 8

KEEP A GOOD HEART. THAT'S THE MOST IMPORTANT THING
IN LIFE. IT'S NOT HOW MUCH MONEY YOU MAKE OR WHAT YOU CAN
ACQUIRE. THE ART OF IT IS TO KEEP A GOOD HEART.

—*Joni Mitchell*

Lemon Meringue Pie

1 (3-ounce) package lemon pudding
    and pie filling mix
1/2 cup sugar
1/4 cup fresh lemon juice
2 egg yolks
2 cups water
1 baked (9-inch) pie shell
4 egg whites
1 teaspoon cream of tartar
1/4 cup sugar

Stir the pie filling mix, 1/2 cup sugar, the lemon juice and egg yolks in a saucepan. Stir in the water. Bring to a boil over medium heat, stirring constantly. Remove from the heat and let cool for 5 minutes, stirring twice. Pour into the pie shell. Combine the egg whites and cream of tartar in a bowl. Beat with an electric mixer at high speed until stiff peaks form. Beat in 1/4 cup sugar gradually. Spread over the filling, sealing to the edge. Bake at 375 degrees for 5 to 10 minutes or until golden brown and the egg white is cooked through. Remove to a wire rack to cool.

Serves 6 to 8

THE GRASS IS NOT ALWAYS GREENER ON THE OTHER SIDE
OF THE FENCE. FENCES HAVE NOTHING TO DO WITH IT. THE GRASS
IS GREENEST WHERE IT IS WATERED.

—*Robert Fulgham*

Key Lime Tart in Coconut Crust

1 cup flaked coconut
1/2 cup gingersnap crumbs
1/2 cup graham cracker crumbs
1/4 cup (1/2 stick) butter, melted
4 egg yolks
1 (14-ounce) can sweetened condensed milk
1 teaspoon grated lime zest
1/3 cup Key lime juice

Mix the coconut, gingersnap crumbs, graham cracker crumbs and butter in a bowl. Press onto the bottom and 3/4 inch up the side of a 9-inch springform pan or pie plate. Bake at 350 degrees for 5 minutes. Remove to a wire rack to cool. Chill until cold. Whisk the egg yolks in a bowl until thick and pale yellow. Add the sweetened condensed milk, lime zest and lime juice. Stir to mix well. Pour into the prepared crust. Chill until firm. Serve with whipped cream.

Serves 6 to 8

NOTE: If raw eggs are a problem in your area, use an equivalent amount of pasteurized egg yolks.

HE WHO CANNOT FORGIVE OTHERS DESTROYS THE BRIDGE

OVER WHICH HE HIMSELF MUST PASS.

—*George Herbert*

Fresh Strawberry Pie

1 cup all-purpose flour
¹/2 cup chopped pecans
¹/2 cup (1 stick) butter, melted
1 cup sugar
3 tablespoons cornstarch
1 cup water
¹/2 package strawberry gelatin
1 pint fresh strawberries, sliced
1 (8-ounce) container frozen whipped topping,
    thawed, or 1 cup whipped cream

Mix the flour, pecans and butter in a bowl. Press onto the bottom and up the side
of a 9-inch pie plate. Bake at 350 degrees for 15 minutes. Remove to a wire rack
to cool completely. Mix the sugar, cornstarch and water in a saucepan. Cook until
thick, stirring frequently. Remove from the heat and stir in the gelatin. Let cool.
Fold in the strawberries. Pour into the cooled crust and spread with the whipped
topping. Chill until ready to serve.

Serves 6 to 8

TO IGNORE THE UNEXPECTED. . .WOULD BE TO LIVE WITHOUT

OPPORTUNITY, SPONTANEITY, AND THE RICH MOMENTS OF

WHICH LIFE IS MADE.

—*Stephen Covey*

Pecan Pie

1/2 cup (1 stick) butter, softened
1 cup sugar
3 eggs, lightly beaten
3/4 cup dark corn syrup
1/4 teaspoon salt
1 teaspoon vanilla extract
2 cups chopped pecans
1 unbaked (9-inch) pie shell
Several pecan halves

Beat the butter in a bowl with an electric mixer. Beat in the sugar gradually and beat until light and fluffy. Stir in the eggs, corn syrup, salt, vanilla and chopped pecans. Pour into the pie shell. Decorate the edge of the filling with pecan halves. Bake at 350 degrees for 40 to 50 minutes. Remove to a wire rack to cool.

Serves 8

Pecan Crunch Pie

3 egg whites
1/2 teaspoon baking powder
1 cup sugar
1 cup graham cracker crumbs
1 cup pecans, chopped
1 teaspoon vanilla extract
1 cup whipping cream, whipped

Beat the egg whites and baking powder in a bowl. Beat in the sugar gradually. Beat until stiff peaks form. Fold in the graham cracker crumbs, pecans and vanilla. Spread in a well-buttered 10-inch pie plate. Bake at 350 degrees for 30 minutes. Remove to a wire rack to cool completely. Chill for 4 to 5 hours. Serve each slice topped with a dollop of whipped cream.

Serves 8

Apple Turnovers

2 cups all-purpose flour
2 tablespoons granulated sugar
2 teaspoons baking powder
1/2 teaspoon salt
3/4 cup cold milk
1/4 cup vegetable oil
6 firm cooking apples, peeled,
   cored and quartered
1/2 cup packed brown sugar
1/2 teaspoon ground cinnamon
1/4 teaspoon nutmeg
6 tablespoons walnuts
Milk
Granulated sugar

Mix the flour, 2 tablespoons sugar, the baking powder and salt in a bowl. Add the milk and oil all at once and stir briskly until the dough forms a ball. Cover and chill. Turn out the dough onto a lightly floured work surface. Pat or roll out the dough to 1/4 inch. Cut into 6 squares. Place 4 apple quarters on each square. Mix the brown sugar, cinnamon and nutmeg in a small bowl. Sprinkle evenly over the apples. Top each with 1 tablespoon of the walnuts. Fold the corners of the dough over the apples and pinch the edges to seal. Place in a buttered baking dish. Brush with milk and sprinkle with sugar. Bake at 350 degrees for 35 to 40 minutes or until the apples are tender.

Serves 6

Bartlett Delight

1/2 cup granulated sugar
1/2 cup packed dark brown sugar
1/4 cup all-purpose flour
1 teaspoon ground cinnamon
1/2 teaspoon nutmeg
4 ripe Bartlett pears, peeled,
    cored and thinly sliced
    (about 3 1/2 cups)
1 tablespoon fresh lemon juice

1 teaspoon vanilla extract
1 (2-crust) refrigerator pie pastry
1/3 cup all-purpose flour
1/4 cup packed dark brown sugar
1/4 teaspoon ground cinnamon
2 tablespoons chilled butter,
    cut into small pieces
1 egg white, lightly beaten

Mix the granulated sugar, 1/2 cup brown sugar, 1/4 cup flour, 1 teaspoon cinnamon and the nutmeg in a bowl. Combine the pears, lemon juice and vanilla in a large bowl. Toss gently to mix. Add the sugar mixture and toss gently to coat. Roll out 1 pie pastry on a lightly floured work surface to remove the fold lines. Place on a nonstick baking sheet lined with foil. Spoon the pear mixture in the center of the pastry, leaving a 3-inch border of dough. Mix 1/3 cup flour, 1/4 cup brown sugar and 1/4 teaspoon cinnamon in a bowl. Cut in the butter with a pastry blender or fork until crumbly. Sprinkle over the pear mixture. Lift the edges of the pastry up over the pear mixture to form a rim, or "bowl." Flute the edges to seal. Roll out the remaining pie pastry on a lightly floured work surface to remove the fold lines. Cut out leaves with a 2 1/2-inch leaf-shape cookie cutter. Arrange the pastry leaves on the pear mixture and brush with the egg white. Bake at 425 degrees for 10 minutes. Reduce the heat to 350 degrees and bake for 35 minutes or until golden brown and bubbly. Let cool for 20 minutes before serving. Serve with whipped cream.

Serves 6 to 8

Bananas Foster

6 tablespoons butter
1/4 cup packed brown sugar
4 ripe bananas, sliced lengthwise
1/2 teaspoon ground cinnamon
1/2 cup banana liqueur
1 cup white rum
4 large scoops vanilla ice cream

Melt the butter in a large skillet. Add the brown sugar and heat until the sugar dissolves, stirring constantly. Add the bananas and sauté until heated through. Sprinkle with the cinnamon. Remove from the heat. Add the banana liqueur and rum and carefully ignite with a long match. Baste the bananas with the flaming liquid until the flames die out. Serve over the ice cream.

Serves 4

FOR I AM CONVINCED THAT NEITHER DEATH, NOR LIFE, NOR ANGELS, NOR PRINCIPALTIES, NOR PRESENT THINGS, NOR FUTURE THINGS, NOR POWERS, NOR HEIGHT, NOR DEPTH, NOR ANY OTHER CREATURE WILL BE ABLE TO SEPARATE US FROM THE LOVE OF GOD IN CHRIST JESUS OUR LORD.

—Romans 8:37-39

Banana Split Cheesecake

1²/3 cups graham cracker crumbs
6 tablespoons butter, melted
32 ounces cream cheese, softened
1¹/4 cups granulated sugar
3 eggs
2¹/2 teaspoons vanilla extract
¹/2 cup granulated sugar
3 tablespoons cornstarch
¹/2 teaspoon salt

1 (20-ounce) can crushed pineapple
1 tablespoon butter
1 large ripe banana
Lemon juice
¹/2 cup pecans, chopped and toasted
Caramel ice cream topping
Chocolate ice cream topping
1 cup heavy whipping cream
¹/4 cup confectioners' sugar

Mix the graham cracker crumbs and 6 tablespoons melted butter in a bowl. Press onto the bottom and 2 inches up the side of a springform pan coated with nonstick cooking spray. Beat the cream cheese in a large bowl with an electric mixer at high speed until light and fluffy. Beat in 1¹/4 cups granulated sugar gradually. Add the eggs 1 at a time, beating well after each addition. Stir in the vanilla. Pour into the prepared crust. Bake at 350 degrees for 40 minutes. Reduce the temperature by 25 degrees if you are using a pan with a dark colored exterior. Turn off the oven and leave the oven door ajar. Let the cheesecake stand in the oven for 30 minutes. Remove from the oven and let cool completely. Cover and chill for 8 hours. Combine ¹/2 cup granulated sugar, the cornstarch, salt, pineapple and 1 tablespoon butter in a saucepan. Bring to a boil, stirring constantly. Boil for 2 minutes, stirring constantly. Remove from the heat and let cool. Chill until cold. Loosen the cheesecake from the side of the pan with a sharp knife and remove the side. Spread the pineapple mixture on top of the cheesecake. Slice the banana thinly and dip the slices in lemon juice. Arrange the banana slices on top of the pineapple mixture. Sprinkle with the pecans and drizzle with caramel topping and chocolate topping. Beat the cream in a bowl with an electric mixer until soft peaks form. Beat in the confectioners' sugar 1 tablespoon at a time. Spread over the top of the cheesecake and garnish with maraschino cherries.

Serves 10 to 12

cherry crunch cake

2 cups self-rising flour
1 cup (2 sticks) butter or margarine, softened
1 cup chopped pecans
1 envelope Dream Whip topping mix,
  prepared according to the package directions
1 (16-ounce) package confectioners' sugar
8 ounces cream cheese, softened
1 to 2 (21-ounce) cans cherry pie filling
1 cup chopped pecans

Mix the flour, butter and 1 cup pecans in a bowl. Press into an oblong baking pan coated with nonstick cooking spray. Bake at 400 degrees for 20 minutes or until golden brown. Cool in the pan on a wire rack. Combine the prepared topping mix, confectioners' sugar and cream cheese in a bowl. Stir to mix well. Spread over the cooled cake. Cover and chill. Spread the pie filling over the cream cheese mixture and sprinkle with 1 cup pecans. Chill until ready to serve.

Serves 10

Oak Hill Delight

1 (21-ounce) can cherry pie filling
1 (20-ounce) can crushed pineapple
1 (2-layer) package yellow cake mix
3/4 cup (1 1/2 sticks) butter, melted
1 1/2 cups chopped pecans
3/4 cup flaked coconut

Spread the cherry pie filling and pineapple in the bottom of a 9×12-inch baking pan coated with nonstick cooking spray. Sprinkle with the cake mix. Pour the melted butter evenly over the top. Sprinkle with the pecans and coconut. Bake at 350 degrees for 45 minutes or until a wooden pick inserted in the center comes out clean. Cool in the pan on a wire rack.

Serves 15

Angel Chocolate Layers

1 1/2 cups all-purpose flour
1/2 cup chopped pecans
3/4 cup (1 1/2 sticks) butter, melted
8 ounces cream cheese, softened
1 cup confectioners' sugar
1 (16-ounce) container frozen whipped
   topping, thawed
2 (3-ounce) packages chocolate instant
   pudding mix
3 cups milk

Mix the flour, pecans and butter in a bowl. Press onto the bottom of a greased
9×13-inch baking pan. Bake at 350 degrees for 20 minutes. Cool in the pan on a
wire rack. Beat the cream cheese and confectioners' sugar in a bowl. Fold in 1/2 the
whipped topping. Spread over the cooled crust. Chill until firm. Beat the pudding
mix and milk in a bowl until thickened. Pour evenly over the cream cheese layer.
Chill until firm. Spread the remaining whipped topping over the pudding layer.
Chill until ready to serve.

Serves 15

THE PROBLEM IS NOT THAT THERE ARE PROBLEMS.
THE PROBLEM IS EXPECTING OTHERWISE AND THINKING THAT
HAVING PROBLEMS IS A PROBLEM.

—*Theodore Rubin*

chocolate Delight

1 (2-layer) package devil's food cake mix,
  batter prepared according to the package directions
1 cup Kahlúa (or to taste)
4 packages chocolate mousse mix,
  prepared according to package directions
1 (12-ounce) container frozen whipped
  topping, thawed
4 chocolate-covered toffee candy bars, crushed

Pour the cake batter into a greased 9×13-inch cake pan. Bake according to the package directions. Remove to a wire rack and let cool slightly. Poke holes in the top of the cake with a fork. Pour the Kahlúa evenly over the cake. Let stand overnight. Crumble 1/2 of the cake into the bottom of a large serving bowl. Top with 1/2 of the mousse. Spread 1/2 of the whipped topping over the mousse and sprinkle with 1/2 of the crushed candy. Repeat the layers to use the remaining cake, mousse, whipped topping and candy. Cover and chill.

Serves 16

WE ARE NOT HUMAN HAVING A SPIRITUAL EXPERIENCE,

BUT SPIRIT HAVING A HUMAN EXPERIENCE.

—Barbara Marciniak

Twinkie Cake Dessert

10 Twinkies, split
2 (10-ounce) packages frozen strawberries, thawed
1 large package instant vanilla pudding mix
1¹/2 cups milk
1 (14-ounce) can sweetened condensed milk
1 (12-ounce) container frozen whipped
topping, thawed

Arrange the Twinkies in a single layer in the bottom of a 9×13-inch baking pan.
Spoon the strawberries evenly over the top. Combine the pudding mix and milk in
a large bowl. Stir to mix well. Fold in the sweetened condensed milk and whipped
topping. Pour over the strawberries. Cover and chill.

Serves 10

Creeping Crust Cobbler

¹/2 cup (1 stick) butter
1 cup self-rising flour
1 cup sugar
¹/2 cup milk
2 cups fresh fruit

Melt the butter in an 8×8-inch baking pan in the oven. Tilt the pan to spread the
melted butter. Sift the flour and sugar into a bowl. Add the milk and stir to mix
well. Pour the batter evenly over the melted butter in the pan; do not stir. Top with
the fruit; do not stir. Bake at 350 degrees for 40 to 60 minutes or until golden
brown. Remove to a wire rack to cool.

Serves 4 to 6

White Chocolate Bread Pudding

4 ounces white chocolate, chopped
2 cups milk or half-and half
1 loaf French bread, torn into small pieces
1 cup sugar
1 (13-ounce) can evaporated milk
4 eggs, beaten
5^{1}/$_{3}$ tablespoons butter, melted
1 teaspoon vanilla extract
White Chocolate Sauce (below)

Combine the chocolate and milk in a saucepan. Cook over low heat until the chocolate melts, stirring often. Combine the bread, sugar, evaporated milk, eggs, butter, vanilla and chocolate mixture in a large bowl. Stir to mix well. Pour into a greased 8×10-inch baking pan. Bake at 325 degrees for 45 minutes. Cool in the pan on a wire rack. Serve with warm White Chocolate Sauce.

Serves 12

White Chocolate Sauce

1 cup milk or half-and-half
1 cup evaporated milk
1 cup sugar
4 ounces white chocolate, chopped
3 tablespoons butter
4^{1}/$_{2}$ teaspoons cornstarch
Water
1 teaspoon vanilla extract

Combine the milk, evaporated milk, sugar, chocolate and butter in the top of a double boiler. Cook over hot water until the chocolate melts, stirring often. Dissolve the cornstarch in a small amount of water in a small bowl. Add to the chocolate mixture. Cook until thickened, stirring constantly. Remove from the heat and stir in the vanilla.

Ultimate Bread Pudding

8 cups torn dry bread
5 eggs, beaten
3 cups sugar
1/2 cup (1 stick) butter, melted
2 cups each half-and-half and milk
1 cup raisins
1 (8-ounce) can crushed pineapple in heavy syrup
1/2 cup flaked coconut
1 cup crushed pecans
1 tablespoon vanilla extract
2 teaspoons butter flavoring
Topping (below)

Spread the bread in a baking pan coated with nonstick cooking spray. Mix the eggs and sugar in a large bowl. Stir in the butter, half-and-half and milk. Stir in the raisins, pineapple, coconut, pecans, vanilla and butter flavoring. Pour over the bread and stir to mix. Let stand for 10 minutes or until the liquid is absorbed. Bake, covered with foil, at 375 degrees for 45 minutes. Uncover and bake for 15 minutes longer or until firm to the touch. Pour the hot Topping evenly over the pudding. Bake for 15 minutes longer. Remove to a wire rack to cool completely.

Serves 10

Topping

1/2 cup (1 stick) butter
1 (14-ounce) can sweetened condensed milk
1 cup half-and-half
1 cup dark rum
1 (6-ounce) package white chocolate bark
1 teaspoon each almond extract and butter flavoring

Combine the butter, sweetened condensed milk, half-and-half, rum, chocolate bark, almond extract and butter flavoring in a saucepan. Cook over low heat until melted and smooth, stirring constantly.

Banana Pudding

1 large package vanilla instant pudding mix
2 cups milk
1 (14-ounce) can sweetened condensed milk
1 cup sour cream
1 (8-ounce) container extra-creamy frozen
  whipped topping, thawed
1 tablespoon vanilla extract
1 box vanilla wafers
5 bananas, sliced

Combine the pudding mix and milk in a large bowl. Beat with an electric mixer until smooth. Add the sweetened condensed milk, sour cream, whipped topping and vanilla. Beat until smooth. Crush a few wafers and set aside. Fit a layer of whole wafers in the bottom of a 12-cup serving bowl. Arrange a ring of wafers upright around the outside edge. Top with a layer of sliced bananas. Cover with the pudding mixture to the top of the outside wafers. Continue layering to use all the whole wafers, bananas and pudding mixture, ending with the pudding mixture. Sprinkle with the reserved wafer crumbs. Cover and chill overnight.

Serves 8 to 10

IF YOU WANT OTHERS TO BE HAPPY, PRACTICE COMPASSION.

IF YOU WANT TO BE HAPPY, PRACTICE COMPASSION.

—The Dalai Lama

caramel Brownies

1/3 cup evaporated milk
1 (14-ounce) package caramels
1 (2-layer) package German Chocolate cake mix
1/2 to 3/4 cup (1 to 1 1/2 sticks) butter, softened
1/3 cup evaporated milk
1 cup chopped pecans
1 cup (6 ounces) chocolate chips

Combine 1/3 cup evaporated milk and the caramels in a saucepan. Cook over low heat until the caramels melt, stirring often; keep warm. Combine the cake mix, butter, 1/3 cup evaporated milk and the pecans in a large bowl. Stir to mix well. Pat 1/2 of the dough into a lightly greased 9×13-inch baking pan. Bake at 350 degrees for 6 minutes. Sprinkle with the chocolate chips. Pour the caramel mixture evenly over the top. Spoon dollops of the remaining dough on the top, pressing the dough lightly into the caramel layer. Bake at 350 degrees for 15 to 18 minutes. Let cool for 1 hour. Cut into squares.

Serves 24 to 30

IN A FULL HEART, THERE IS ROOM FOR EVERYTHING, AND IN AN

EMPTY HEART THERE IS ROOM FOR NOTHING.

—*Anonio Porchia*

Chewy Pecan Squares

4 eggs, beaten
2 cups biscuit mix
1 tablespoon heavy cream or evaporated milk
1 teaspoon vanilla extract
1 (16-ounce) package dark brown sugar
2 cups chopped pecans

Combine the eggs, biscuit mix, cream, vanilla and brown sugar in a 2-quart glass measuring cup or microwave-safe bowl. Stir to mix well. Microwave on High for 2¹/₂ minutes and stir. Microwave on High for 3¹/₂ minutes, stirring every minute. Stir in the pecans. Pour into a 9×9-inch baking pan well coated with nonstick cooking spray. Bake at 350 degrees for 40 minutes. The surface will appear sticky. Let cool for 30 minutes. Cut with a warm knife.

Serves 8 to 12

NOTE: These are best if made 1 day ahead.

THE WAY YOU GET MEANING INTO YOUR LIFE IS TO DEVOTE

YOURSELF TO LOVING OTHERS.

—Morrie Schwartz

Pecan Clusters

3 tablespoons butter
3 cups coarsely chopped pecans
12 ounces white almond bark, cut into pieces

Melt the butter in a 10×15-inch baking pan in the oven. Tilt the pan to spread the melted butter. Spread the pecans evenly over the melted butter. Bake at 300 degrees for 30 minutes, stirring every 10 minutes. Remove the pan to a wire rack. Place the almond bark in a large microwave-safe bowl. Microwave on Defrost until melted. Add the pecans and stir to coat. Drop by spoonfuls onto waxed paper. Cool until firm.

Makes 4 dozen clusters

NOTE: You may wish to place newspaper under the waxed paper to avoid marring the counter.

Pralines

3 cups sugar
3 cups pecans
1 (12-ounce) can evaporated milk
1/2 cup (1 stick) butter
Pinch of salt
3 tablespoons light corn syrup
1 tablespoon vanilla extract

Combine the sugar, pecans, evaporated milk, butter, salt, corn syrup and vanilla in a saucepan. Bring to a gentle boil, stirring often. Remove from the heat and beat until creamy. Drop by tablespoonfuls onto waxed paper.

Makes about 2 dozen pralines

contributors

Helen Aaron, *In memory of Faye D. Aaron, Jean Buatt*

Carmen Abou-Issa

Angella Aldridge

Beverly Angelle, *In memory of Theresa LeVasseur*

Annie Arnold, *In memory of Roy Arceneaux, Sister Therese Remy, Nola Wilson, Linda Goff*

Marilyn Arton, *In memory of Mrs. Gerry Allen*

Charles (Spike), Sid, John & Patrick Axtell, *In memory of Sid Wheeler*

Moe Axtell Roberts, *In memory of Elizabeth Ann Patout Alting*

Tab Benoit, *In memory of Anatole "Nat" Babin*

Lewis Bernard, *In memory of Stella Tinsley*

Becky Berthelot, *In memory of Albin Major, Van Major*

Marcelle Bienvenu, *In memory of Rhena Bienvenu*

Malou Blair, *In memory of Roy Blair*

Kathi Bordlee, *In memory of Evan "Jay" Wood, Marshall Stockstill, Joneen Guidry*

Elda Boutte, *In memory of Momma A*

Becky Brackin, *In memory of Laura Landreneau*

Joan Broussard, *In memory of Brad Broussard, Luda Bernis Theriot*

Betty Broussard, *In memory of Mr. and Mrs. Eugene G. Broussard, Mr. & Mrs. Hebraud Perry, Josha Jade Broussard, Stephen Broussard, Dwight and Streeter Broussard*

Ed Mae "Maw" Broussard

Sally Bruno, *In memory of Tookie Juneau*

Adrienne Callender, *In memory of M.O. Blanchard, Sr.*

Shirley Callender, *In memory of Jimmy Callender & Hazel LaCoste*

Vickie Carney

Lona Carroll, *In memory of Georgia Rutherford*

Margaret Chamberlain, *In memory of Olivia Henry, Rubbie Chaisson, Amy Kelly*

Jane Claibourne, *In memory of Helen Peters, Doug Claibourne*

Rob Clarke, *In memory of Eldon Arceneaux*

Gussie Clause, *In memory of Aline Prejean*

Denise Cole, *In memory of Oral, Pearl & Sherman Morgan, Zelma Morgan Kirby, Pat Moore, Bud Morgan*

Jolynn Cole, *In memory of Carolyn Serio*

Sue Cole, *In memory of Jeanette Cole*

Leisa Comeaux, *In memory of Dorothy House*

Faith & Perry Comeaux, *In memory of Walter & Maria Conklin, Ecton & Betty Curole*

Australia Comeaux, *In memory of O'Neil Comeaux*

Ginger Comeaux

Nancy Connick, *In memory of Libby Connick*

Gerry Cormier, *In memory of Mary Ann Kern*

Dianna Courville, *In memory of Dorothy O'Blanc Royer*

Becky Credeur, *In memory of Kay Kasischke, Warren Axtell, Russell Credeur*

Clint Crowe, *In memory of Charlie*

Ann and Dr. Wayne Daigle

Gail Daigle, *In memory of Rita Daigle*

Dee Daigle, *In memory of Marian Daigle*

John Daigre, *In memory of Lee Hill*

Irma Darphin, *In memory of Eula Muller*

Wilma D. Dartez, *In memory of Livia Davis, Stanley F. Davis*

Beverly Daspit, *In memory of Mrs. Avery G. Landry*

Melba Axtell Debaillon, *In memory of Ola Keller, Kay Kasischke*

Hazel Delahoussaye, *In memory of Ida Duplechain Dupre*

Delores Dubois

Andy Simon Ducharme, *In memory of J. Raymond Simon*

Sandra Duhon, *In memory of Richard Blanchat, Frances Marron*

Daisy Dupuy, *In memory of Donna & Mitchell Hodges, Edmond & Edna Grow, Wanda Janise, Leslie Lancon, Earl Beadle*

Rev. Robert Eastwood, *In memory of Kitty Sue Eastwood*

Simon Eid, *In memory of Farida Eid*

Virginia Elliott, *In memory of Weldon Dow Elliott*

Betty Ellison, *In memory of Betty Wright, E. W. Wynne*

Mary Ethridge, *In memory of Nettie A. Garon*

Dona Faulkinberry, *In memory of Willard Dugas, Edley Broussard*

Cynthia Fernandez, *In memory of Anne Provost*

Darlene Flynn

Carolyn Fontenot, *In memory of Louis Labbé*

Lee Forgey, *In memory of Joyce Fouquier*

Deborah Fortier, *In memory of Margot Fortier, Emily Samuels*

Sandra Fox, *In memory of Owen Blanchard*

Grace Frederick, *In memory of Kermit Doucet*

Catherine Fridley, *In memory of Evelyn Wiltz*

Cindy Frugé, *In memory of D.L. Fusilier*

Linda Gaffney, *In memory of Jim Gaffney*

Monique Girard, *In memory of Kenneth J. Patin*

Janice Gist

Baby Givens, *In memory of Marguerite Fertitta Serafino*

Charlie Goodson, *In memory of Nel Broussard*

Jan Greer, *In memory of Mrs. Joseph Troville*

June Griffith

Anne Maria Guidry, *In memory of Sarah Culotta*

Peggy Guillory, *In memory of Ned N. Guillory, W. B. Underwood*

Dana Guthrie, *In memory of Billy Roznavok, Marie Fontenot*

Beverly Broussard Hains

Michael Halphen, *In memory of Mr. Edgar Halphen*

Dorothy Hampton, *In memory of J.P. Hampton*

Fran Hampton, *In memory of Frank Cangelosi*

Nita Harrington, *In memory of Flora Killmer Henderson*

Meda Hayne, *In memory of Don Hayne*

Carol Hebert, *In memory of Bobby Hebert*

Kim Higdon, *In memory of Marie Estelle Blanchard*

Marilyn Hoffpauir, *In memory of Betty Hyatt*

Dianne Hoyt & Max Hoyt, *In memory of Gertrude Sellers Broussard, Keith Broussard, & J. B. Broussard*

Madelyn Hoyt, *In memory of Wilmer Hoyt*

Susan Key, *In memory of Dr. Kieran J. Key*

Nouphay Kongphongmany

Shirlyn Laborde, *In memory of Amos Trahan*

Allen LaBry

Pauline Lalande, *In memory of Melva Dugas*

Angel Lanclos, *In memory of Annie Vidrine*

Mary Landgrave, *In memory of Gene Matherne, Michael Landgrave*

Amy Landry, *In memory of Louis Labbé*

Donna Rita Landry, *In memory of Myrna Fox, Jo Ann Penton*

Jodi Landry State Farm

Pat Landry, *In memory of Peter Russo, Mrs. Roy Broussard, Jeanne Landry, Yvonne Gooch*

Paulette Landry, *In memory of Lenora Guidry, Louis Labbé*

Flo Landry

Dianne Langlinais

Mrs. Ed Lanier, *In memory of Mr. & Mrs. Peter Berteau*

E.D. "Doc" Lanier, *In memory of Mr. & Mrs. Donald Lanier, Alma, Gloria & Herbert Lanier, Jude Guillory, Louis Miller, Mr. & Mrs. B. J. Parent*

Corbett LeBouef, *In memory of Harry LeBouef*

Elinor Lee, *In memory of Paul Lee, Elinor Schussler*

Pat LeJeune, *In memory of Lillian Schmersahl*

Wayne & Colleen Lemoine, *In memory of John and Warren Bruce*

Emma D. Lerille, *In memory of Livia Davis, Stanley F. Davis*

Melanie Livingston, *In memory of Dub Livingston, Bill Fields*

Sue Mannina, *In memory of Chess, Essie & Jeanard Fontenot, Gayle Guchereau, Trey Mannina*

Ann Marmanoe

Juliet Thibeaux McKay, *In memory of Marguerite Ellen Thibeaux*

Adele Meier, *In memory of Margo Comeaux*

Krista Meier

Erin Meyers, *In memory of Emelda and "Red" Aldrich*

Angie Miller

Gabriella Mills

Dr. Joni Orazio and Dr. Charles Bramlet, *In Memory of Sugar, The Foin, Bramlet, Olivier, Granger & Primeaux Families*

Jeannie Oubre

Dianna (Dee) Patin, *In memory of Kay Kasischke, Elizabeth Dartez*

Eugene Patout, *In memory of Elizabeth Ann Patout Alting*

Arleen Picard, *In memory of Morris & Laura Belle Morvant and Ed Picard*

Susan Picone, *In memory of Myrtis Hebert, Wilbert V. Picone*

Carla Pommier, *In memory of Jeffrey Herring*

Susan Prejean, *In memory of George Bartell*

Tierny Robertson, *In memory of Reno Robertson*

Jennifer Rollins, *In memory of Raymond Simon*

Jean Rosen

Joanne Samanie, *In memory of Betty Chauvin*

Carleen and Sandy Sandoz, *In memory of Gay Sandoz*

Susan Savoie, *In memory of Donald Savoie, Sr.*

Cindy Schiller, *In memory of Mr. & Mrs. Byron Schiller*

Kelly Scofield, *In memory of Florence Ruzas, Ethel Fruge*

Kathy Scott, *In memory of Weldon Elliott*

Tou Sengsourivong

Anna Claire Seymour, *In memory of E. Rupert Campbell, Sr.*

Molly Shealy, *In memory of Johnny Shealy, Jay Henderson*

Jalaine Shirley, *In memory of Raymond Simon*

Jennifer Sibille, *In memory of Mary Ann Davis*

Ra Nelle Simon, *In memory of J. Raymond Simon, Aunt Julie, Angeline Touchet (R. Simon's mother)*

Shannon Simon-Iler, *In memory of J. Raymond Simon*

Jane Smith, *In memory of Albin Major*

Carol Stewart, *In memory of Helen Pitt*

Kathy Randol Stokley, *In memory of Rusty Randol & Arthur Randol*

Melba Stoute, *In memory of Charle R. Stoute*

Paula Swearingen, *In memory of Johnnie Craig*

Lelia Tanner, *In memory of "Cappy" Schiller*

Theresa Thompson, *In memory of Anne Provost*

Linda Touchet, *In memory of Louise Durio*

Susanna Trilling

Debbie Tweedel, *In memory of Shirley Guilbeau*

Lucille Venable, *In memory of Ferdie Venable*

Beth Viguerie

Jayne Vildibill

Sandy Walsh, *In memory of Joe Walsh*

Claire Ward, *In honor of all the wonderful work that Hospice of Acadiana does*

Pat Warnken, *In memory of Richard Warnken*

Index

To order additional copies of

Angels in the Kitchen,

call (337) 237-1332, ext. 1132 or 1133,

or visit our Web site,

www.hfacadiana.com.